Learn Bridge in One Hour

Learn in 10 Easy Steps
Play from the first step!

By Samir Riad

To order additional copies, please contact
BookSurge, LLC
www.booksurge.com
1-866-308-6235
orders@booksurge.com

Learn Bridge in One Hour

By Samir Riad

Edited by Christopher Wilder

Layout by Amy Sirota

To Alex, Julia, and Sophia.

Table of Contents

Introduction

Congratulations, you have just made the most important step toward learning Bridge! You bought my book, and for that I thank you and I promise you, you will learn the game in no time, and have great fun playing it.

When I wanted to get together with friends and family to play Bridge, I was often missing one player, sometimes two. My wife and I wanted to increase the number of people in our circle of friends that knew how to play Bridge, so we invited couples to our house for a meal and Bridge, with the promise that they'd learn how to play Bridge in one evening.

The challenge was finding a way to teach Bridge in a short time – an hour or less – so we could have time to play before the evening was over. I came to discover after lots of practice the basic steps to learning Bridge in one hour. I tried my approach with many of our friends. All reported that they learned the game and loved being able to play right away.

This book provides you with 10 steps to learning Bridge. Instead of applying all Bridge rules at once, we will start with simple play and then add more sophistication to it, step by step. Before you know it, you will be playing proper Contract Bridge, and know all the rules.

If you have never played Bridge before, this is the book for you. You can even sit at the table with three other players that have never played bridge before, follow the given steps and you'll all learn at the same time. You can always repeat a step until you're confident enough to proceed to the next.

Each chapter represents one basic step. You can read straight through this book in advance, and be perfectly well prepared to play, or, use my approach and go directly to "playing the step" at the end of each chapter. Read it, follow the instructions, and start playing the step right away. Then go to the next chapter, and play step 2, then 3... you get the idea. Play step by step at your own speed.

You don't have to memorize anything in such a short time, just use the reference tables provided in each section to guide you through bidding, scoring, and playing the hand. Later on, previous non-Bridge players can read through all of the chapters in the book and gain a greater understanding of the game. For most people this book is all you need to learn how to play bridge.

You are not going to be a highly skilled player in one hour, but you'll learn the basics of the game. You'll learn how to make a bid and how to play the hand. This book will definitely get you started.

What you'll need next is practice and more practice.

If you know how to play Bridge, you still need this book. It will help you teach your friends quickly, with enough time left in your evening for you all to play and enjoy the game.

Bridge is fun and should not be taken too seriously. Maybe you have heard about angry arguments erupting during bridge games. This doesn't need to happen. This book does offer a section on "Bridge Etiquette" that helps reduce the possibility of conflicts, but, for the most part, if you start with a desire to enjoy a challenging game with your friends and family you will have a great time!

So, as you're getting ready to start on your Bridge adventure, sit back, relax and enjoy the greatest card game ever invented!

GETTING STARTED

You need two decks of playing cards, one red and one blue, or any other two different colors. The four players sit around the table so that every two players are opposite each other. Everybody takes turn dealing the cards clockwise, and the player across from the dealer always shuffles the 2nd deck and puts it on his right (the left of the next dealer).

All players could either be playing for the first time, or you could have a mix of Bridge players and newcomers. If some players already know how to play the game, they still need to follow the ten steps in order to allow the first timers to learn.

This method is the best way to teach your friends how to play Bridge and increase the number of Bridge players in your pool of friends and family. The more Bridge players around, the easier it is to find 3 other players to play with you.

The Object of The Game

1. You need four players to play Contract Bridge.

2. Each two players that sit opposite each other are partners.

3. The play begins with "bidding". Each team will bid to win a certain number of tricks.

4. The team that bids the highest plays offense. The team scores points if they make their bid.

5. The team that lost the bidding plays defense and scores points if they prevent the other team from making their bid.

6. You win or lose a Bridge match as a team. The team with the most points wins.

STEP 1
FOLLOW THE SUIT: HIGHEST CARD WINS

What you need to know:

1. The deck of cards has 52 cards

2. There are four suits in the deck, Spades (♠), Hearts (♥), Diamonds (♦), and Clubs (♣). They rank in that order where Spades is the highest rank and Clubs is the lowest rank.

3. Each suit consists of 13 cards. Ace (A), King (K), Queen (Q), and Jack (J), which are also called the 4 honors. Then 10, 9, 8, 7, 6, 5, 4, 3, and 2. The rank is in this order where the Ace is the highest and the 2 is the lowest.

4. A trick is a round of four cards, where each player played one card.

5. It takes four players to play Bridge. Each two players sitting across from each other are partners, and they add up their tricks together. North and South are partners. West and East are partners.

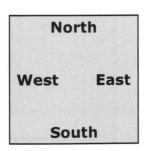

♠   ♦   15

Starting the game:

Each player draws a card from the deck. The two highest cards partner together and the two lowest cards partner together. The player with the highest card deals, chooses the deck of cards, and chooses where to sit.

North and South are partners, and West and East are partners.

The dealer (D) distributes the cards to each player one card at a time starting from the left. You deal clockwise around the table until all the cards are dealt. Now each player has 13 cards.

Each player should organize his cards in suits. Starting with the Spades on the left, then Hearts, Clubs, and Diamonds. The suits are also organized in alternate colors, black, red, black, and red. It's easier to see the cards this way.

Example of organizing your hand:

♠ A K J 9 3 ♥ Q 9 5 ♣ A Q 2 ♦ 10 4

Now you are ready to play the first hand. The player to the left of the dealer plays a card in any suit and the other players must play the same suit as long as they have cards in that suit. The player with the highest card in that suit wins the first "trick". Remember that a trick is a round of four cards where each player played one card.

The winner plays next. The partner that wins the first trick keeps all the winning tricks at his side of the table in a neat pile face down. When you take additional tricks, neatly pile these cards on top of your last trick but separate the tricks enough so you can easily see how many tricks you've taken. The winner of the trick leads from his hand in any suit and everybody must follow the same suit. The highest card wins.

If a player does not have a card in the played suit, he can discard in any other suit. The discarded card can never win even if it's the highest card.

When all the cards are played, the hand is completed. There are a total of 13 tricks in each hand. Each partnership count their tricks, the one with the highest number of tricks wins the hand.

The next player on the left deals the next hand. The dealing goes clockwise regardless who won the last hand. You can repeat step 1, if you like, until you are ready for step 2.

Bridge Tip

At the beginning of the Bridge game, each player draws a card from the deck. The two highest cards partner together and the two lowest cards partner together. The player with the highest card deals, chooses the deck of cards, and chooses where to sit.

Test yourself

Questions:

1. How do the four suits rank in Bridge?
2. How many cards is each player dealt?
3. What constitutes a trick in a Bridge hand?
4. How many total tricks in the hand?

Answers:

1. Spades (♠), Hearts (♥), Diamonds (♦), and Clubs (♣). They rank in that order where Spades is the highest rank and Clubs is the lowest rank.
2. 13 cards
3. A trick is a round of four cards, where each player played one card.
4. 13 tricks.

♠ ♦

Playing Step 1

- Each player draws a card from the deck. The two highest cards are partners, and the two lowest cards are partners. The player with the highest card is the dealer.

- Each two partners sit across each other as North and South, or West and East.

- The dealer distributes the cards, one card at a time until the whole deck is dealt.

- The player on the left of the dealer plays the first card in any suit.

- All other players must follow the suit. The highest card wins the first round of four cards. This round of play is known in Bridge as a trick. The winner of a trick places the four cards in front of him face down in a neat pile. Additional tricks are placed on top of the last trick but separated enough so that you can easily tell how many tricks you have won. One partner keeps all the tricks.

- The winner of the trick leads from his hand in any suit and everybody follows the suit.

- If you are out of the played suit, you discard in any other suit.

- When you discard, you can't win the trick even if you discard an Ace.

- When all the cards are played, the hand is completed.

- The partnership with the highest number of tricks wins the hand.

STEP 2
PLAY WITH A TRUMP SUIT

What you need to know:

1. Any one of the four suits could be a Trump suit. A trump card is like a wild card. It beats any other card in the deck except for a higher trump.

2. If it's your turn to play, and you are void in the played suit, you can trump the trick and win it with a trump card.

3. The trump card always wins even if it's not the highest card, unless trump cards are played against each other.

4. You do not have to play a trump card if you are void in the suit that was led. You don't want to trump your partner's card if it is high and will win the trick.

5. The trump in this step will be chosen randomly. It will be the trump of the last card dealt.

In **step 2**, the dealer distributes the cards one at a time until they are all distributed same as in **step 1**. Only this time he puts the last card in the middle of the table and turn it over face up and its suit becomes the trump for this hand. The dealer then returns the card to his hand before start of play.

In the early years of Bridge, the game was called Whist and this was how they chose the trump suit before the game was more developed.

Bridge Tip

In the early years of Bridge, the game was called Whist and they picked the trump suit by turning the last card dealt face up. Its suit became trump for this hand. This was how they chose the trump suit before the game was more developed.

The player on the left of the dealer leads by playing the first card. You play the hand just like **step 1**, only now you can trump. The winner of the first trick plays the next card.

If you are out of the suit being played, you can trump it and win the trick with one of the trump cards in your hand. Somebody else can trump over you with a higher trump card and win.

Partners should not compete against each other. If one of the partners is going to win the trick with a King, there is no need for the other partner to put the Ace on top of the winning King.

You don't have to trump the trick if you don't want to, and you don't trump your partner's winning trick. You can simply discard any other card instead.

If somebody leads with a trump, then you follow suit just the same as you would do for any other suit.

Since the total number of tricks in each hand is 13 tricks, then in order for your partnership to win the hand, you should win the majority of the 13 tricks, which is 7 tricks or more. The winner always wins more than 6 tricks, so in Bridge we call the first 6 tricks "book" and we count your winning tricks over book.

There's only one winner because there's only one team that can win more tricks than book. You score 1 when you win 1 trick over book. You score 2 when you win 2 tricks over book and so on. Note the winning team and how many tricks over book they scored.

If you like, repeat **step 2** a few times until you get used to playing with trump cards.

Bridge Tip

Any one of the four suits could be a Trump suit. A trump card is like a wild card. If you are void in the played suit you can trump the trick and win it, even with the smallest trump card.

♣ ♥

Test yourself

Questions:

1. Which suit can be trump suit?
2. When is it appropriate to trump?
3. How many tricks is "Book"?
4. After the hand is played, who deals the cards next?

Answers:

1. Any one of the four suits can be the trump suit.
2. When it's your turn to play and you are void in the played suit.
3. 6 tricks.
4. The player on the left of the previous dealer.

Playing Step 2

- The player on the left of the previous dealer will deal this hand. After all the cards are distributed, the last card is put in the middle of the table face up. The suit of this card is the trump suit for this hand. A trump card is like a wild card. It beats any other card in the deck except for a higher trump. The dealer returns the trump card to his hand.

- The cards of the trump suit are special cards because if you are void in the played suit you may trump the trick and win it, even with the smallest trump card.

- The player on the left of the dealer plays next and follows the suit just like **step 1**. You always follow the suit if you have it and, if the trump suit is led, you play it just like any other suit. The trump suit is only special when it's not led and is used to trump the trick.

- When two players trump the same trick, the one with the highest trump card wins.

- Remember you're playing as a team with your partner. Do not trump your partner's winning high cards.

- When all the cards are played, the hand is completed.

- Since the total number of tricks in each hand is 13 tricks, the winning team will have to win more than half the tricks, or more than 6 tricks.

- In Bridge the first 6 tricks are called "book" and the winning team always wins more than book.

- If the winning team wins 7 tricks, it means book plus 1. It's understood that scoring 1 means you have won 7 tricks. If you score 3 it means you have won 9 tricks, book plus 3.

- Note the winning team and how many tricks over book they scored.

STEP 3
THE OPENING BID

What you need to know:

1. The object of bidding is to communicate with your partner and to figure out the strengths and weaknesses of your combined hands.

2. In order to determine the strength of your hand, you need to count your points. Count both your honor points (Ace, King, Queen and Jack), and your distribution points (void, singleton and doubleton).

3. The four honors have a point value. The Jack is 1 point, the Queen is 2 points, the King is 3 points, and the Ace is 4 points.

4. To help you remember the point value of the 4 honors, think of how the cards rank starting from the 10. What comes after the 10 is the Jack (11), then the Queen (12), then the King (13), and then the Ace (14). The points value of the 4 honors correspond to their position after the 10, 1 for the Jack, 2 for the Queen, 3 for the King, and 4 for the Ace.

5. If you have the four honors in any suit, that equals to 10 points.

6. There are four suits in the deck of cards, so the total honor points in the game are 40.

7. In addition to the Honor points, there are also distribution points. If you don't have a card in any suit (Void), that's 3 points. If you have only one card in any suit (Singleton), that's 2 points. If you have only two cards in any suit (Doubleton) that's 1 point.

♠   ♦

8. In order to open in one of the 4 suits, the player needs to have 13 or more "Honor & Distribution" points. If you want to open in No Trump, you should have 16-18 points, all in honor points, plus balanced distribution. When you play No Trump you play the hand just like step 1.

9. When your bid is 1 Club, it means that you bid to win 1 trick over book (7 tricks) when the trump is Clubs. If you bid 2 Spades, it means that you bid to win 2 tricks over book (8 tricks) when the trump is Spades. If you bid 1 No Trump, it means that you bid to win 1 trick over book (7 tricks), when the trump is No Trump.

Honors	Points
Ace (A)	4 points
King (K)	3 points
Queen (Q)	2 points
Jack (J)	1 points

Distribution*	Points
Void	3 points
Singleton	2 points
Doubleton	1 points
*Not used in No Trump bids.	

Opening 1 in a Suit:

You need 13-21 points (total honor and distribution points) and 5 cards or more to open 1 in a suit. If you have 13-15 points it is considered a low opening, while 19-21 points is a high opening.

Each player picks his best suit to open with. It could be Spades, Hearts, Diamonds or Clubs. Any suit is fine. Your best suit is the longest suit (the suit with the most cards). The minimum requirement in the opening suit is 5 cards and at least 2-3 honors. The idea is to have enough strength in your opening suit to win 2½ fast tricks. The four honors are Ace, King, Queen and Jack. The 10 is always considered the fifth honor although it doesn't have point value. Below are some practice hands showing 1 suit opening.

♠ A K Q J 2
♥ 9 5
♣ A Q 2
♦ 10 4 3

Honor points: 16
Distribution points: 1
5 cards in Spades
Bid: 1 Spade

♠ K 9 3
♥ A K Q 9 5
♣ A Q 2
♦ 10 4

Honor points: 18
Distribution points: 1
5 cards in Hearts
Bid: 1 Heart

♠ K 9 3
♥ Q 9 5
♣ A K Q J 2
♦ 10 4

Honor points: 15
Distribution points: 1
5 cards in Clubs
Bid: 1 Club

♠ A J 9
♥ Q 9 5
♣ A 2
♦ K Q J 10 9

Honor points: 17
Distribution points: 1
5 cards in Diamonds
Bid: 1 Diamond

♠ A K 10 9 5
♥
♣ K J 7 2
♦ A 8 4 3

Honor points: 15
Distribution points: 3
5 cards in Spades
Bid: 1 Spade

♠ K 9 3
♥ A K 10 9 5
♣ Q 9 2
♦ 10 4

Honor points: 12
Distribution points: 1
5 cards in Hearts
Bid: 1 Heart

♠ K 9 3
♥ Q 9 5
♣ A Q J 8 2
♦ 10 4

Honor points: 12
Distribution points: 1
5 cards in Clubs
Bid: 1 Club

♠ J 9 7 2
♥ Q 9 5
♣ A
♦ K Q 10 9 5

Honor points: 12
Distribution points: 2
5 cards in Diamonds
Bid: 1 Diamond

Bridge Tip

In order to open 1 in any suit, you need 13-21 points, and 5-cards or more in that suit. If you have 2 similar suits, always choose the longest one. Choose a major suit over a minor suit. If you have two equal major suits, bid the Heart first.

Opening 2, in a Suit:

To open 2 in a suit you must have 21-25 points, and 5-7 cards in that suit. Below are some practice hands showing 2 suit's opening.

♠ A K Q J 5 3
♥ A K
♣ K Q 7
♦ 10 4

Honor points: 22
Distribution points: 2
6 cards in Spades
Bid: 2 Spades

♠ A K 10 9
♥ A K Q 9 5
♣ A Q 5 2
♦

Honor points: 22
Distribution points: 3
5 cards in Hearts
Bid: 2 Hearts

♠ 5
♥ A K 5
♣ A K Q J 8 7
♦ K J 10

Honor points: 21
Distribution points: 2
6 cards in Clubs
Bid: 2 Clubs

♠ K 9
♥ A K 5
♣ Q 2
♦ A K Q J 10 4

Honor points: 22
Distribution points: 2
6 cards in Diamonds
Bid: 2 Diamonds

Opening 3, in a Suit:

Opening 3 in a suit requires 6-10 honor points and a long suit of 7 cards or longer. The reason that you can bid so high with so few honor points is that you can anticipate that most of your trump cards, even your low ones, will win tricks because you have so many of them. There's a lot more to opening 3 in a suit but you don't have to go through that right now. You can wait until you learn more Bridge technique and then come back to read this section.

Opening 3 in a suit is a pre-emptive bid because it can disturb the bidding and can take playing the hand away from your opponents. You use a pre-emptive bid to stop your opponents from winning the game, or drive them to bid at a higher level than they're comfortable with.

To figure out if you can open 3 or more, count your winning tricks then add 2 more tricks if you have a game (vulnerable*), or add 3 if you don't have a game (not vulnerable). The 2 and 3 represent the number of tricks you estimate that your partner will win. They also represent how much you can afford to lose if your partner couldn't win any tricks. Although sometimes you can make your pre-emptive bid, many times you don't, and you most likely will get doubled by your opponents.

As you will see in **Step 7** "Keeping the score", when you are vulnerable, and doubled, going down 2 will cost you 500 points penalty. This is the same as going down 3 when you're not vulnerable. 500 points should be all the risk you're allowed to take when you open with a pre-emptive bid. Otherwise it might not be worth it. Another advantage to this bid is it sometimes discourages your opponents from bidding all together. They may be uncomfortable starting their first bid at the 3rd or 4th level.

A team becomes (vulnerable) after scoring their 1st game. They are subject to higher penalties when they fail to make their bid and higher bonuses when they win. Not vulnerable means that they haven't scored a game yet. At that stage no extra penalties and no extra bonuses.

Below are some practice hands showing 3 suits openings.

♠ 10 9	♠ K 10 9
♥ 5	♥ 7
♣ K Q J 10 8 7 6 2	♣ 7 2
♦ 8 4	♦ A J 10 9 8 6 4

Honor points: 6
Distribution points: 4
8 cards in Clubs
Bid: 3 Clubs

Honor points: 8
Distribution points: 3
7 cards in Diamonds
Bid: 3 Diamonds

Opening in No Trump:

If the bidder doesn't have a 5 card opening suit but has at least 16-18 points (all honor points), balanced distribution (no void, no singleton), and 3 suits are protected by high honors, he can open
1 No Trump*.

Balanced distribution means the cards are divided 4-3-3-3, or 4-4-3-2, or 5-3-3-2. Three suits protected means you have 1 or more winners in each of the 3 suits. In order to open 2 No Trump, you need 22-24 points, with all 4 suits are protected by high honors. To open 3 No Trump, you should have 25-27 points and all suits protected as well. On page 37 are some examples of No Trump openings.

*Playing without designated trump suit.

Bridge Tip

The highest opening at the "one" level is 1 No Trump. It requires:

- *16 – 18 points: All honors points.*
- *Balanced distribution: No void, no singleton, and the cards are divided 4-3-3-3 or 4-4-3-2 or 5-3-3-2.*
- *Three suits protected: 1 or more winners in each of the 3 suits.*

♣   ♥

♠ K Q 9 3
♥ K J 8
♣ 10 4 2
♦ A Q 10

Honor points: 15
Distribution points: 0
Balanced distribution
Bid: 1 No Trump

♠ K Q 9
♥ A K Q 9
♣ A Q 2
♦ A 10 4

Honor points: 24
Distribution points: 0
Balanced distribution
Bid: 2 No Trump

♠ A K 9 3
♥ A K Q 9
♣ A Q 2
♦ A 4

Honor points: 26
Distribution points: 0
Balanced distribution
Bid: 3 No Trump

Making the next bid:

If the dealer makes an opening bid, and it's your turn to bid next, what will you bid? If you have opening bid as well, you make a bid but your bid must be higher than the previous bid.

The bidding always progresses by going up like an auction. When a player opens, the next player must bid higher. You can't win an auction by bidding lower. You always go higher.

Bidding goes up both in rank of the suits and in levels. The four suits rank in alphabetical order from the lowest to the highest: Clubs, Diamonds, Hearts, and Spades. "No Trump" ranks higher than Spades and is the highest "suit" bid in the game.

The levels are numbers one, two, three, etc. The first level is the "one" level; 1 Club, 1 Diamond, 1 Heart, 1 Spade, and 1 No Trump from lowest to highest in that order. The "two" level is: 2 Clubs, 2 Diamonds, 2 Hearts, 2 Spades, and 2 No Trumps, in that order. You go up the levels and the suit ranks until 7 No Trump which is the highest bid possible in the game. In **Step 3** we are not going up very high, just one round of opening bids.

♠   ♦

Refer to the "opening bid" table in this chapter for a summary to the various opening bids.

Your hand:

♠ A K J 9 3
♥ Q 9 5
♣ A Q 2
♦ 10 4

Honor points: 16
Distribution points: 1
5 Cards in Spades
Bid: 1 Spade

Example of opening bid:

In the above hand, you open 1 Spade because you have enough opening points. You total 17 points, 16 honor points and 1 distribution point (Doubleton in Diamonds). Your best suit is Spades because you have 5 Trumps in Spades. You open 1 Spade.

In **Step 3** we are only focusing on opening bids and only the players with opening points are allowed to bid. As you will see in later chapters, once a player has made an opening bid the bidding rules "change". However, in the examples below each player will have a chance to bid once or say pass. The dealer starts the bidding if he has opening points (13 or more). If he doesn't, he passes.

The bidding goes clockwise around the table until all players have a chance to bid and there have been 3 passes in a row. The player with the highest opening bid wins the bid and his trump will be the trump for this hand. The player to his left leads the first card.

♣ ♥

Example 1:

♠ A K J 9 3
♥ K J 8 7
♣ 8 5
♦ A 3

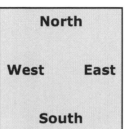

♠ 8 5
♥ A 10 4
♣ A Q J 9 2
♦ K Q 10

♠ 7 6 4
♥ 6 3
♣ K 7 6 3
♦ J 8 6 5

♠ Q 10 2
♥ Q 9 5 2
♣ 10 4
♦ 9 7 4 2

South (Dealer)	West	North	East
5 points	17 points	18 points	5 points
No suit	5 card suit	5 card suit	No suit
Pass	1 Club	1 Spade	Pass

South dealt, has only 5 points, said pass
West Has 17 points, 5 cards in Clubs, opens 1 club
North has 18 points, 5 cards in Spades, opens 1 Spade
East has 5 points, said pass

End of one round bidding.
North is the bid winner.
The Trump will be Spades.
North will play 1 Spade, and he'll have to win 1 trick
over book (7 tricks) to make his bid.

♠   ♦   39

Example 2:

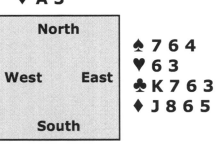

♠ A K J 9 3
♥ K J 8 7
♣ 8 5
♦ A 3

North

♠ 8 5
♥ A 10 4
♣ A Q J 9 2
♦ K Q 10

West   **East**

♠ 7 6 4
♥ 6 3
♣ K 7 6 3
♦ J 8 6 5

South

♠ Q 10 2
♥ Q 9 5 2
♣ 10 4
♦ 9 7 4 2

North (Dealer)	East	South	West
18 points	5 points	5 points	17 points
5 card suit	No suit	No suit	5 card suit
1 Spade	Pass	Pass	2 Clubs

North dealt, Has 18 points, 5 cards in Spades,
opens 1 Spade
East has 5 points, said pass
South has 5 points, said pass
West has 17 points, 5 cards in Clubs, bids 2 clubs

End of one round bidding.
West is the bid winner.
The Trump will be Clubs.
West will play 2 Clubs, and he'll have to win 2 tricks
over book (8 tricks) to make his bid.

♣   ♥

Example 3:

♠ A K J 9 3
♥ K 8 7
♣ 8 5
♦ A 3

	North	
♠ 8 5		♠ J 7 2
♥ A 4 2		♥ J 3
♣ A Q J 9 2	West East	♣ K 7 6 3
♦ K Q 10		♦ J 8 6 5
	South	

♠ Q 6 4
♥ Q 9 5
♣ 10 4
♦ 9 7 4 2

West (Dealer)	North	East	South
17 points	16 points	7 points	5 points
5 card suit	5 card suit	No suit	No suit
1 Club	1 Spade	Pass	Pass

West dealt, has 17 points, 5 cards in Clubs,
opens 1 Club.
North has 16 points, 5 cards in Spades, said 1 Spade
East, and South passed.

End of one round bidding.
North is the bid winner.
The Trump will be Spades.
North will play 1 Spade, and he'll have to win 1 trick
over book (7 tricks) to make his bid.

♠   ♦   41

The table below will summarize the proper opening bids depending on the strength in your hand.

Table 1: Opening Bids

Opening	Points	Suit	Comments
1 suit (Low opening)	13- 15		Choose a major suit over a minor suit. If you have two equal major suits, bid the Heart first.
1 suit (High opening)	19-21	5 card suit	
2 suit (Demand bid)	21-25	5-7 card suit	Opening two is a demand bid. Your partner must not say pass until a game is reached.
3 suit (Pre-emptive)	6-10 Honor Points	7 card suit or longer	Count your quick tricks, and add 2 if vulnerable, or add 3 when not vulnerable.
1 No Trump	16-18	No void, no singleton. Three suits protected.	Balanced distribution 4-3-3-3, or 4-4-3-2, or 5-3-3-2
2 No Trump	22-24	No void, no singleton. Four suits protected.	Balanced distribution
3 No Trump	25-27	No void, no singleton. Four suits protected.	Balanced distribution

Test yourself

Questions:

1. If you have the four honors in any suit, how many points is that?

2. If you are void in one suit, singleton in another, and doubleton in another suit, how many distribution points is that?

3. What are the required points that you need to open one in a suit or to open one in No Trump?

4. What is the requirement of opening 3 in a suit?

Answers:

1. 10 points. The Ace is 4, the King is 3, the Queen is 2, and the Jack is 1.

2. 6 points. 3 points for void, 2 points for singleton, and 1 point for doubleton.

3. You need 13 – 21 "honor and distribution" points to open 1 in a suit. You need 16-18 Honor points to open 1 in No Trump.

4. Opening 3 in a suit requires 6-10 honor points and a long suit of 7 cards or longer.

Playing Step 3

- In **step 1**, we played the hand with no trump. In **step 2**, we played with a trump suit that was picked randomly. In **step 3**, we will play with a trump suit but this time we will pick the trump through one round of bidding.

- After the cards are dealt, players organize their hand and count both their honor points and their distribution points.

- The four honors are Jack, Queen, King, and Ace. Their points value correspond to their rank after the 10. The Jack comes 1st, and has 1 point value, the Queen comes 2nd, so it has 2 points value, the King comes 3rd with 3 points value, and the Ace comes 4th with 4 points value.

- The distribution points are: Void (out of a suit) equals 3 points, singleton (only 1 card in a suit) equals 2 points, and doubleton (only 2 cards in a suit) equals 1 point.

- In order to open 1 in any suit, you need 13-21 points and 5 or more cards in that suit. If you have 2 similar suits, always choose the longest one. In order to open 2 in a suit you must have 21-25 points, and 5-7 cards in that suit. Refer to Table 1 on page 42, the "opening bids" table, for various opening bids.

- You need 16-18 honor points and balanced distribution to open in No Trump. You need 22-24 honor points to open 2 No Trump. When you open in No Trumps you must not count your distribution points, only count your honor points.

- All players with an opening hand can open. Only one round of bidding is allowed at this step. The player with the highest opening wins the bidding and his trump becomes the trump for this hand.

- If the highest opening suit is "No Trump", then you play the hand with no trump.

- The player on the left of the bid winner (the Declarer) leads by playing the first card.

- Everybody plays the hand just like **step 2** until all 13 tricks are played.

- Note the winning team and how many tricks over book they scored.

STEP 4
RESPONDING TO
THE OPENING BID

What you need to know:

1. The object of bidding is to communicate with your partner and figure out the strengths and weaknesses of your combined hands.

2. Correct opening and responding bids help find your team's best trump and the number of tricks you can score with that trump.

3. When you bid, you promise to win a certain number of tricks (over book) at the trump you choose.

4. The team that promises the highest number of tricks at the highest rank of trump is the bid winner.

In step 4 we will bid two rounds of opening bids and responding bids. Everybody will have a chance to speak twice. Any player with opening hand can open and his partner can respond to his opening bid. The dealer starts the bidding and it goes around the table clockwise. At the end of the 2nd round, 3 players should say pass in a row and end the bidding.

♠   ♦

Responding to 1, in a suit:

Responding to a one suit opener is the most common response in Bridge. If you have less than 6 points you should pass. If you have opening hand of 13-15 points you should jump up a level to signal your strength to your partner. Below are the three options that you have when you respond to 1 suit opening.

Option 1: If you have 3 trump cards in the opening suit, and 6-10 points, respond in the opening suit. If the opening bid was 1 Heart your response bid should be 2 Hearts. The reason behind this bid is the trump count. Your partner opened with 5 trumps. If you have 3, then your total trump count is 8 which is enough to play the hand in this trump suit if you wish.

Option 2: Your second option is to bid a suit of your own. In that case you need at least 4 cards in that suit and 7-10 points.

Option 3: If you can't respond in the opening suit and you don't have a suit of your own, but you have 6-10 points, you bid 1 No Trump. Your partner will understand that you have some points but no 3 cards in his opening suit and no strong 4 card suit of your own.

Bridge Tip

You must have:

*1) 6-10 points and 3 trumps
to respond in the opening
suit, or*

*2) 7-10 points and a 4 card
suit to respond in a new
suit, or*

*3) 6-10 points and no suit to
respond 1 No Trump.*

Examples of responding bids to 1 suit opening:

Option 1:	Option 2:	Option 3:
Opening Bid	**Opening Bid**	**Opening Bid**
1 Heart	1 Club	1 Heart
<u>Your hand:</u>	<u>Your hand</u>	<u>Your hand</u>
♠ A 9 3	♠ A K 10 8	♠ A K 5
♥ Q 9 5	♥ J 10 8 7	♥ 10 7
♣ K 6 2	♣ 9 7	♣ 9 8 7 2
♦ 10 8 5 2	♦ Q 10 4	♦ J 10 4 2
9 points Support in Hearts No biddable suit	11 points Not enought Clubs Biddable Spade suit	9 points Not enough Hearts No biddable suit
Your response	**Your response**	**Your response**
2 Heart	**1 Spade**	**1 No Trump**

Responding to an opening 2 bid in a suit:

If your partner opens 2 of a suit it is called a "demand bid". You can't respond with a pass to a 2 opening bid even with 0 points. The reason is that your partner has so many points (21-25 points), in most cases he can make more than two on his own. Therefore you need to keep the bidding going. You must respond, and keep responding, until a game is reached.

Use the same bidding response strategy as for an opening 1 bid in a suit. Respond by bidding your partners suit, a suit of your own or if you don't have any suit to bid respond with 2 No Trumps. Jump up a level when you have opening hand of 13-15 points. For example, if your partner opens two Hearts and you have a strong Diamond hand with 13 – 15 points,

♣   ♥

respond with a 4 Diamond bid. This tells your partner both your point total and your strongest suit.

Responding to 3, in a suit:

When your partner opens 3 in a suit, it means he has 6-10 points and at least 7 cards in that suit. He can win 6 to 7 tricks from his hand alone. If you have 10 or fewer points you should pass. Your partner is hoping that you can win 2 to 3 tricks in your hand which should just allow your partner to make his bid and no more. If you have an opening hand you should raise the bid in his suit.

Other Examples of response bids:

Option 1:	Option 2:	Option 3:
Opening Bid	**Opening Bid**	**Opening Bid**
2 Diamonds	**3 Clubs**	**1 Spade**
<u>Your hand:</u>	<u>Your hand</u>	<u>Your hand</u>
♠ K 9 7	♠ A 9 3	♠ K Q 9
♥ 10 7 5 2	♥ K 10 7 3	♥ A 9 5
♣ Q 2	♣ Q 9 7 2	♣ Q 10 6 2
♦ J 10 4 2	♦ A 4	♦ A 8 7
7 points	14 points	15 points
Strong Diamonds	Strong Clubs	Strong Spades
No biddable suit	Biddable Heart suit	Biddable Club suit
Your response	**Your response**	**Your response**
3 Diamonds	**5 Clubs**	**3 Spades**

♠ ♦   51

Bridge Tip

If your partner opens 2 of a suit it is called a "demand bid". You can't respond with a pass to a 2 opening bid even with 0 points. The reason is that your partner has so many points that in most cases he can make more than two on his own. You should keep the bidding going until a game is reached.

The table below shows you the various response bids to suit opening:

Table 2: Suit Response Bids

Opening	Response	Comments
1 suit (13-21)	6-10 points, and no biddable suit: bid 1 No Trump.	When you bid No Trump, count only the honors points, not the distribution points.
	6-10 points & 3 Trumps: respond 2 in the opening suit. 13-15 points: jump to the next level forcing a game.	Even if your partner has a low opening of 13 points, if you have 13 points that's 26 total, and enough for a game.
	7-10 points & 4 cards or more in a new suit: respond in the new suit. 13-15 points: jump up a level.	Choose a major suit over a minor suit. If you have two equal major suits, bid the lower rank first.
2 suit (21-25)	0-6 points: bid 2 No Trumps. 7 points plus: bid any Trump. You must keep responding until game is reached.	Opening two is a demand bid. You must not say pass even with 0 points.
3 suit (6-10)	7-10 points: pass, 13-15 points: respond 4 or 5 in the opening suit. (see Step 5)	Think that your partner can make 6-7 quick tricks. How many can you add from your hand?

Responding to 1 "No Trump" Opening:

When your partner opens 1 in a suit, it could be low opening of 13-15 points, or high opening of 19-21 points. You really don't know, and unless you have 6 points or more in your hand, you should pass. On the other hand, when your partner opens 1 No Trump, it is easy to figure it out. It always means 16-18 points and even distribution. No guess, no mess.

♠ ♦

Even with 0 points in your hand, you shouldn't respond with a pass to 1 NT opening. Playing 1 no trump might not be a good idea especially with your weak hand. The best response with 0-7 points is bidding your longest suit of 5+ cards even if your longest suit has no honors.

If your longest suit is Clubs, you respond 2 Clubs. With 10+ points, you jump to 3 Clubs.

Responding to 2 "No Trump" Opening:

If your partner opens 2 NT, that means he has 22-24 points and even distribution. With 4-8 points in your hand, you should go to 3 NT.

In the next chapter "Bidding For A Game", the number of points in bidding and responding will make more sense to you and they will be easier to remember. You will be able to understand the logic behind the point count.

Responding to 3 "No Trump" Opening:

When your partner opens 3 NT, that is enough for a game using only his hand strength, 25-27 points. If you have 8-12 points, you can go immediately to slam. 8-9 points are enough for 6 NT (small slam), and 12 points are enough for 7 NT (grand slam). We will go through the details of NT slam bidding in Step 10. For the time being, please refer to table 3 on page 55 for various NT response bidding.

The table below shows you the various response bids to No Trump opening:

Table 3: NT Response Bids

Opening	Response	Comments
1 No Trump (16-18)	0-7 points, and long suit of 5+ cards: respond 2 in your long suit even with no honors. 10+ points: jump to 3 No Trump	Even if you have 0 points you must respond to 1 No Trump with your longest suit.
2 No Trump (22-24)	4-8 points: respond 3 No Trump	Even if your partner has 22 points, your team has enough for a game.
3 No Trump (25-27)	7 points: bid 4 No Trump, 8-11 points: bid 6 No Trump, 12 points: bid 7 No Trump.	Just add your points to your partner's points, and it will be easy to bid. 26 points are enough for 3 NT, with 33 points bid 6 NT, and with 37 points bid 7 NT.

Examples of responding bids to "No Trump" opening:

Opening Bid 1 NT	Opening Bid 2 NT	Opening Bid 3 NT
Your hand	**Your hand**	**Your hand**
♠ Q J 5	♠ K 9 7	♠ K 9 7
♥ 10 7	♥ 10 7 5 2	♥ 10 7 5 2
♣ 9 8 7	♣ Q 2	♣ Q 10 6
♦ J 10 8 4 2	♦ J 10 4 2	♦ A 8 7
5 points	6 honor points	9 points
5+ cards in Diamonds	No biddable suit	You can win 3 tricks
Bid your long suit	No void, no singleton	No void, no singleton
Your response 2 Diamonds	**Your response** 3 NT	**Your response** 6 NT

♠   ♦

Bridge Tip

When your partner opens 1 in a suit, it could be low opening of 13-15 points, or high opening of 19-21 points. You really don't know, and unless you have 6 points or more in your hand, you should pass. On the other hand, when your partner opens 1 NT, it is easy to figure it out. It always means 16-18 points and even distribution. No guess, no mess.

Opening The Dummy's Hand:

After the player on the <u>left</u> of the Declarer leads, the Declarer's partner becomes the "Dummy". He opens his cards, puts them on the table face up, and does not participate in playing the hand. The Declarer will play both his hand and his partner's hand.

The Dummy lays the cards down one suit at a time starting with the trump on the left then the highest opposite color, then he alternates the last two colors.

If the trump was Spades, then the Dummy lays down his cards as shown in the figure below.

<u>Dummy's Hand:</u>

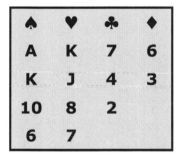

♠	♥	♣	♦
A	K	7	6
K	J	4	3
10	8	2	
6	7		

You play the hand just like the previous step. The trick winner always leads the next card. If the Dummy wins the trick, the Declarer plays from the Dummy.

Bridge Tip

When your partner opens 3 NT, that is enough for a game using only his hand strength, 25-27 points. If you have 8-12 points, you can go immediately to slam.

8-9 points are enough for 6 NT (small slam), and 12 points are enough for 7 NT (grand slam).

The Declarer will be able to look at his cards and the Dummy's cards at the same time, which gives him great control over playing the hand. I will explain in detail the skills of playing the hand in Step 8, but right now here are some quick tips:

1. If you are playing a trump contract, collect the trumps first to prevent the defender from trumping your winners.

2. You can play a suit from the Dummy that is void in your hand and win the trick by trumping it. That is called ruffing. If you can do it both ways, it's called crossruffing.

3. If you have a ruffing or crossruffing opportunity, you might want to delay collecting the trumps until you cash in some ruffing.

4. If you are playing a no trump contract, you want the defenders to collect their winning tricks first. That will establish long suit winners for you and enable you to get the hand back while you still have high honors.

Every trick the Declarer is short of what he bid is called "one down". If he's short two tricks, it's called "two down", and so on. You will learn later that each down has a penalty and, if you are closer to winning the match, those penalties are very high.

At the end of the hand, count how many tricks each team won just for your reference. Don't count scores yet.

Bridge Tip

If you are playing a trump contract, collect the trumps first to prevent the defender from trumping your winners. If you are playing a No Trump contract, you want the defenders to collect their winning tricks first. That will establish long suit winners for you and enable you to get the hand back while you still have high honors.

Test yourself

Questions:

1. What are the minimum points you should have to respond to 1 in a suit?
2. In responding to 1 NT, do you choose the suit with the most honors or the suit with the most cards?
3. Why is opening 2 considered a demand bid?

Answers:

1. 6 points.
2. Respond in your longest suit even with no honors.
3. It's a demand bid because you can't respond with a pass to a 2 opening even with 0 points.

Playing Step 4

- In **step 4**, every player will have a chance to bid twice. The dealer starts the bidding, and it goes around the table clockwise for two rounds or until it ends when 3 players pass in a row, whichever comes first.

- Since 1 suit opening is the most common opening in Bridge, the response to 1 suit opening is the most common response. If you perfect it, then you have learned a great deal about bidding.

- When you respond to 1 suit opening, you have 3 options:
  - Either respond in the opener suit
  - Bid a new suit of your own, or
  - Respond in neither suit by bidding 1 NT.

- You must have 6-10 points and 3 trumps to respond in the opener suit
  - 7-10 points, and 4 cards suit to respond in a new suit, or
  - 6-10 points and no suit to respond 1 NT. Refer to table 2 on page 53.

- When you bid, you always bid higher than the previous bidder.

- At the one level, 1 Club is the lowest bid, then 1 Diamond, then 1 Heart, then 1 Spade, then 1 No Trump.

- If somebody opens 1 No Trump, then the next bid must go to the "two" level – 2 Clubs for example.

♣   ♥

- The team with the highest bid wins the contract. The winning partner that spoke first in the trump suit is the Declarer. The player on his left leads the first card.

- After the lead, the Declarer's partner becomes the "Dummy" and opens his cards. The Declarer plays both his hand and the Dummy's hand until all tricks are played.

- At the end of the hand, the Declarer counts his tricks.

STEP 5
BIDDING FOR A GAME

What you need to know:

1. The scoring system in Bridge greatly affects the way you bid a hand.

2. One of the important elements in Bridge play is to score a "game". Winning a game is a key milestone towards winning the "rubber" (Two game set). What a game is, and how you score one, will become clearer as you read this chapter.

3. In earlier chapters we described that bidding is a way for you and your partner to decide how many tricks you can make. For example, if the final bid of a hand is 3 Hearts, the team that wins the bid is saying that they can make 3 tricks over book (9 tricks) with Hearts as trumps.

4. The tricks have a point value and this is crucial in the scoring process. Spade and Heart tricks (major suits) equal 30 points each. Diamond and Club tricks (minor suits) equal 20 points each. The first no trump trick equals 40 points, then 30 points for each no trump trick after that. The table on page 66 shows you the trick value of each suit.

♠   ♦

Trick Values

Suit	Trick Value
No Trump	40 points*
Spade	30 points
Heart	30 points
Diamond	20 points
Club	20 points

* For the 1st trick then 30 for each following trick.

5. It takes 100 points to score a game. You need to score 4 tricks over book (10 tricks) in Spades or Hearts to win a game in a major suit. You need to win 5 tricks over book (11 tricks) in Diamonds or Clubs to win a game in a minor suit. However, you only need 3 tricks over book (9 tricks) in no trumps to win a game in NT.

The table below shows how many tricks are needed to score a game.

Enough Tricks for a Game	Total Points
3 No Trumps (40+30+30)	100
4 Spades (4x30)	120
4 Hearts (4x30)	120
5 Diamonds (5x20)	100
5 Clubs (5x20)	100

In **step 5** you will learn how to bid for a game. You need to score two games in order to win the rubber (another milestone in winning a bridge match). The two games don't have to be in sequence. You could win a game and that will be 1 game to 0, then your opponents can win a game, and that will be 1 game to 1. Once you or your opponent wins a second game, the rubber is over, and the winner collects the bonus for the rubber. You can also win the rubber with 2 games to 0.

Bridge Tip

It takes 100 points to score a game. You need to score 4 tricks over book (10 tricks) in Spades or Hearts to win a game in a major suit. You need to win 5 tricks over book (11 tricks) in Diamonds or Clubs to win a game in a minor suit. However you only need 3 tricks over book (9 tricks) in No Trumps to win a game in NT.

Game Points:

According to the common wisdom, you must have in your hand and your partner's hand a total of 26 points and even distribution to make a 3 No Trump game, or 26 points and total of 8 trump cards to make 4 in a major suit (Spades or Hearts), or 29 points and 8 cards for 5 in a minor suit (Diamonds or Clubs).

Game	Points
3 No Trumps (9 tricks)	26
4 Spades (10 tricks)	26
4 Hearts (10 tricks)	26
5 Diamonds (11 tricks)	29
5 Clubs (11 tricks)	29
6 small slam (12 tricks)	33
7 grand slam (13 tricks)	37

When you bid in No Trumps, only count your honor points. In all other suits, count both your honor and your distribution points.

If you bid and score 6 in any suit, that's called a small slam. You will receive a small slam bonus. If you bid and score 7 tricks in any suit, that's called a grand slam and is the highest score in Bridge. You will receive a grand slam bonus. Don't worry about scoring a slam at this point; let's first learn how to score a game.

When you have enough points for a game, you should always bid for a game. If you don't have enough points to bid a whole game, stop at a partial game. Although making a game is more desirable than a partial game, don't get caught in a trap of reaching beyond your points and then finding yourself not making your bid (going down) most of the time.

The Logic of The Points:

The total number of honor points in the deck of cards is 40 points. If one of the two teams got all the 40 points they should be able to win all the tricks. If the points are divided equally, each team has 20 points, then each team should be able to make half the tricks. Half of 13 tricks is 6½, or approximately 7 tricks, which is book plus 1.

So, with the points divided equally, every team should be able to make 1 in a suit. With good distribution, a team can make 2 or even 3 in a suit. But that is it. You and your partner will not make a game if you and your partner have only 20 points. You need at least 6 more points to bid and make a game in No Trumps or in a major suit.

Making 3 No Trump game (9 tricks) requires 26 points. Making a game in a major suit (10 tricks) also requires 26 points. However, making a game in a minor suit (11 tricks) requires 29 points to make up for the extra trick. Remember Spades and Heart are major suits while Clubs and Diamonds are minor suits.

Bridge Tip

You must have in your hand and your partner's hand a total of 26 points and even distribution to make a 3 No Trump game, or 26 points and total of 8 trump cards to make 4 in a major suit (Spades or Hearts), or 29 points and 8 trump cards to make 5 in a minor suit (Diamonds or Clubs).

Below are some points distribution that will not result in a game for any of the two teams.

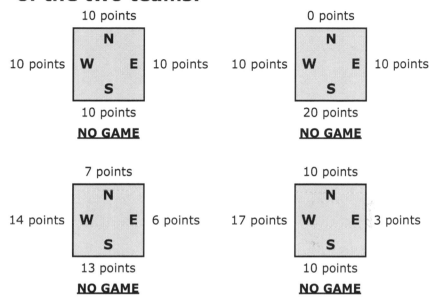

10 points		0 points	
10 points — N / W E / S — 10 points		10 points — N / W E / S — 10 points	
10 points		20 points	
NO GAME		**NO GAME**	

7 points		10 points	
14 points — N / W E / S — 6 points		17 points — N / W E / S — 3 points	
13 points		10 points	
NO GAME		**NO GAME**	

Below some possible game examples where one of the teams got enough points for a game.

5 points		11 points	
18 points — N / W E / S — 11 points		5 points — N / W E / S — 2 points	
6 points		22 points	
GAME W&E		**SLAM N&S**	

♠ ♦

Bridge Tip

When you have enough points for a game, you should always bid for a game. If you don't have enough points to bid a whole game, stop at a partial game. Although making a game is more desirable than a partial game, don't get caught in a trap of reaching beyond your points and then finding yourself not making your bid (going down) most of the time.

More game examples:

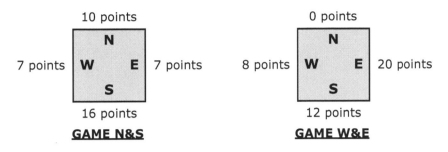

The Four Bids:

When you communicate with your partner through bidding, always use the point system and you'll get it right. Here's the terminology for the first round of bidding as it goes around the table:

1. Opening bid: First player to open
2. Overcall: First bid by opponent (not pass)
3. Respond to opening bid
4. Respond to overcall bid

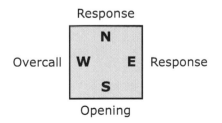

In step 5, assume that West and East will say pass and let's focus on the opening bid by South, the response to the opening bid by North and re-bidding in order to reach a game, or stop at a partial game.

The players will use Bridge bidding rules. One means book plus one, and two means book plus two. Maximum bid is book plus 7, which is equal to 13 tricks and that is equal to all the tricks in the hand.

Refer to the re-bid table 4 on pages 77 and 78, and take a moment to think after the first round of opening and responding. See if you can figure out how many points your team has, and what is the best trump for your team.

If you don't have enough points for a game, you must stop at a partial game at the "one" level or the "two" level. There's no point to bid any higher and make it more difficult on your team to make your bid. When you stop at a partial game, you still need to stop at the best trump for your team.

If you have enough points for a game, then bid for a game once you know your team's best trump suit. Use the re-bid table as a reference for the various re-bidding options. You will see the opener re-bid and the response to the re-bid. Most of the time, you can wrap up the bidding after the second round. The common wisdom is, the less you talk the less your opponent will know about your cards and your partner's cards.

The rules are very simple – you want to stay in a suit with a total of 8 or more cards in your team's hands. If everybody follows the opening and responding rules, it's easy to estimate the total number of cards your team has in the bid suit.

You want to go to game when you have enough points for the game. The toughest opening for your partner to figure out is opening 1 in any suit. Your partner will not know if you have low opening (13-15 points), or high opening (19-21 points). Only you know. So, when you open 1, you will be the one adding up the points and deciding whether or not your team should go to game.

Before you decide to play No Trump, make sure you have balanced distribution and stoppers (winners) in all four suits. When you open 1 No Trump, you must have 3 suits protected by sure winners. If your partner takes you to a No Trump game, he must have the fourth suit protected.

Partial Game:

It happens very often in Bridge that the two partners stop at a partial game for lack of strength. Scoring a partial game is a good thing. You can always reach a game the next time you're playing the hand. For example, if you stop at 2 Spades that's 60 points. All you need the next time you play the hand is 40 more points to finish the game.

A partial game has disadvantages. It can be erased by your opponents when they score a game. That's why you stop at a partial game only when you have to. It's always better to go for a game when you can.

Bridge Tip

The toughest opening for your partner to figure out is opening 1 in any suit. Your partner will not know if you have low opening (13-15 points), or high opening (19-21 points). Only you know. So, when you open 1, you will be the one adding up the points and deciding whether or not your team should go to game.

Table 4: Re-Bid

Opening	Response	Opener re-bid	Responder re-bid
1 suit (13-21)	6-10 points, and no suit: bid 1 No Trump	Respond 2 in the opening suit	Pass
	6-10 points & 3 Trumps: respond 2 in the opening suit. 13-15 points: jump to the next level forcing a game	Add up your team points, if enough for a game, go to game. Otherwise pass, there is no benefit to raising the bid.	Pass
	7-10 points and 4 cards or more in a new suit: respond in the new suit. 13-15 points: jump to the next level	Play partner's new suit if you have 4 cards. Re-bid your opening suit if you have 6+ cards. Bid a secondary suit with 4+ card suit.	Make sure you don't leave your team playing a suit with less than 8 cards in Trump. If two suits are equal, choose the major suit.
2 suit (21-25)	0-6 points: bid 2 No Trumps. 7 points plus: bid any Trump. Must keep responding until game is reached	If your partner says 2 No Trump, go to your secondary suit	Go back to opening suit with 3+ cards. Bid the secondary suit with 4+ cards.
3 suit (6-10)	7-10 points: pass. 13-15 points: go to game	Pass	

Table 4: Re-Bid, cont.

Opening	Response	Opener re-bid	Responder re-bid
1 No Trump (16-18)	0-7 points, and long suit of 5+ cards: respond 2 in your long suit even with no honors. 10+ points: jump to the next level.	With 2 suit respond, pass if you have 3 Trumps. If your partner jumps to the next level, go to game.	Pass
2 No Trump (22-24)	4-8 points: respond 3 No Trumps	Pass	Pass
3 No Trump (25-27)	7 points: bid 4 No Trumps. 8-11 points: bid 6 No Trumps. 12 points: bid 7 No Trumps	Against 4 No Trumps, pass or go to slam with 33 team points or more.	

Test yourself

Questions:

1. How many trick points are required to reach a game?

2. What is a rubber?

3. How many honor and distribution points should your team have to score a game in a major suit and in a minor suit?

4. What is the requirement in playing a game in No Trump?

5. When does a partial game get erased?

Answers:

1. 100 points.

2. The winning of two games.

3. 26 points to score a game in a major suit and 29 points to score a game in minor suit.

4. 26 honor points, balanced distribution and stoppers in all four suits.

5. A partial game gets erased when the opponents score a game.

Playing Step 5

- Refer to the Re-Bid table 4 on pages 77 and 78, and start the bidding. Once a player opens, opponents will pass throughout the bidding.

- The two partners will bid, respond, and re-bid according to the re-bid table, until they finish bidding either at a game or partial game and 3 players say pass in a row.

- For the sake of practicing bidding for a game, if the two players stopped at a partial game, shuffle the cards and deal again.

- Once a team bids a game, then play the hand.

- The first player to bid in the trump suit plays the hand and becomes the Declarer. His partner becomes the Dummy.

- First player to lead is the player on the left of the Declarer, and then the Dummy opens his cards and lays them down.

- The Declarer plays the hand and tries to make his bid. The defenders will try to get him down.

- After all the tricks are played, count the Declarer's winning tricks over book.

STEP 6
THE OVERCALL BID

What you need to know:

1. Once your opponent opens the bidding, and you make a bid rather than passing, it is called an overcall bid.

2. An overcall bid is similar to the opening bid but the bidding rules are slightly different. It requires 10-15 points to overcall an opening at the 1 level.

3. At the two level, you are required to have normal opening points of 13-15 points in order to overcall.

4. Another example of an overcall bid is to say "double". This "double" has a different meaning than the traditional "double" that is used by a player when he is pretty sure that his team will prevent his opponents from making their bid.

5. Using "double" as an overcall bid is a way to tell your partner that you have opening hand and to ask your partner for his longest suit.

6. Even if you know that you will end up playing defense, the overcall bid is useful to tell your partner your strong suit and what to lead to you.

7. Overcall bids are also used to confuse the bidding, to raise the level of the bidding, and to make it harder for the opening team to quickly find and bid their strongest suit.

♠   ♦

In step 6, all players will be allowed to bid and re-bid according to the bridge rules.

In the next table, <u>Table 5: Overcall Bid</u>, you will see most of the overcall options and the overcall responses. You now have all the tables necessary for bidding.

1. Opening bids table (Table 1)

2. Responding bid tables (Tables 2 and 3)

3. Re-bid table (Table 4)

4. Overcall bid table (Table 5)

You can use these tables during bidding until you don't need them anymore and can bid on your own. These tables are also at the end of this book in the Reference Tables section. When I play Bridge, what helps me remember how to bid is my point count, and then my team total point count. When I bid, I tell my partner how many points I have. When my partner responds, he tells me how many points he has. Opening and responding in any suit, at any level is only a vehicle to communicate the total points in your team's hand. By the time you know the total points you already know the best trump for your team.

Table 5: Overcall Bid

Overcall	Suit	Comments	Response
1 suit (10-15 points): overcall at the 1st level.	5 card suit with 2+ top honors. (Aces, Kings, or Queens)	At the one level, you can overcall with as low as 10 points.	6-10 points and 3 Trumps: respond 2 in the overcall suit. 13-15 points: jump to the next level not forcing a game.
2 suit (13-15 points): overcall at the 2nd level.	5 card suit with 2+ top honors. (Aces, Kings, or Queens)	At the two level, you must have opening points to overcall.	6-10 points and 3 Trumps: respond 3 in the overcall suit. 13-15 points: go to game.
1 No Trump (16-18 points)	The opponent's opening suit must be well protected. It means you should have 1 or 2 sure winners in your opponent's opening suit.	You must be prepared to play it, if you have to. Also must have balanced distribution 4-3-3-3, or 4-4-3-2, or 5-3-3-2	0-7 points, and long suit of 5+ cards: respond 2 in your long suit even with no honors. 10+ points: jump to the next level.
Double (13-16 points) "Take-Out Double"	Support in the unbid suits. Or 5 card suit with 2+ top honors. (Aces, Kings, or Queens)	It's a call to your partner to name his best unbid suit. Preferably a major suit, and better stay at low level.	8-10 points, name your best unbid suit. Preferably a major suit. 8-10 points, with balanced distribution, and a stopper (sure winner) in the opponent's suit bid 1 No Trump. 13+ points: go to game.

Table 5: Overcall Bid, continued

Overcall	Suit	Comments	Response
3 suit or more (pre-emptive), (6-10 points) plus 7+ cards in one suit. Usually to stop your opponents from scoring a second game and winning the rubber.	7+ card suit	Before you bid, count your quick tricks, and add 2 if vulnerable*, or add 3 when not vulnerable**. Might get a double, and might go down.	7-10 points: pass. 13-15 points: go to game.

GENERAL BIDDING TIPS:

Get to the point ASAP

Wrap up your bidding ASAP. For example, if you open 1 Spade and your partner responds with 2 Spades, count your team's points - if they are 26 or more, bid 4 Spades and finish the bidding. Now your opponents only know that you have Spades and they have to guess everything else.

If you don't have enough for a game, stay at low level

You open 1 Spade with 14 points and your partner responded 2 spades with 6-10 points. That's 24 points at the most. Not enough for a game. You pass. There is no point of going higher. If you can't get a game, two Spades or 3 Spades are the same. They are both a partial game.

* Vulnerable: already won a game.
** Not Vulnerable: have not won a game yet.

Open 5 card suits or longer

Besides having the necessary points, you need 8 trumps total to play in any suit. You should have 5 trumps minimum when you open and your partner should have 3 trumps minimum when he responds in your suit.

Choose your Opening Suit

If you have two suits, each 5 cards, open in the major suit. If you have two 5 card major suits, open in the lower one. For example, if you have Hearts and Spades open in Hearts. You can always go up to the Spades later. This is also true in minor suits. If you have Clubs and Diamonds, open in Clubs. You can always go up to the Diamonds later.

Open according to your points, no more, no less

When you open, don't over bid and don't under bid. It will mislead your partner. If you confuse your partner with your opening bid you run a great risk of either settling for a partial game when you could have scored a game, or you over bid and go down. The secret to winning in Bridge is to open correctly.

Test yourself

Questions:

1. What is the minimum number of points you are required to have in order to overcall on the 1 level and at the 2 levels?

2. When your partner overcall bid is "double", what does it mean?

3. Traditionally, how many Trump cards should you have in order to open in a particular suit?

4. If you have two major suits that are equal in strength (each with 5 cards), which one should you open with?

Answers:

1. On the 1 level you are required to have minimum 10 points to overcall. At the 2 level, a minimum of 13 points is required.

2. It means that your partner has opening points and is asking you for your longest suit.

3. 5 trump cards.

4. The lower rank. You can always go to the higher rank later.

Playing Step 6

- The dealer starts bidding. Once a player opens, opponents will either pass or overcall.

- Refer to the overcall table (Table 5 on page 83). If you have the required points and distribution, make an overcall bid.

- The partner to the opener will respond to the opening bid and the partner to the overcall bidder will respond to the overcall bid.

- The bidding will go around the table until 3 players say pass in a row.

- The contract winners play offense. The first player to bid the trump suit plays the hand and becomes the Declarer. His partner becomes the Dummy.

- The first player to lead is the player on the left of the Declarer.Then the Dummy opens his cards and lay them down.

- The Declarer plays the hand and tries to make his bid. The defenders will try to get him down.

- After all the tricks are played, count the winning tricks.

STEP 7
KEEPING THE SCORE

What you need to know:

1. Everyone should know how to keep the score in Bridge. Knowing how the scoring system works is crucial to the bidding process.

2. The score pad is divided into two columns, one for each team. "We" indicates the team that is keeping the score, with "They" being the other team. The score pad also has a horizontal line dividing the pad into an upper section and lower section. Some of the score is written over that dividing line and some written under the line.

3. When you make your bid, you receive points for your contracted tricks under the line. That could be for a full game or partial game. If you get overtricks they will be scored above the line.

4. The Declarer get penalized for not fulfilling his contract. The penalty points go to the opponents and are written above the line.

5. When you receive any bonuses for the rubber, for a slam, for having 4 honors in one suit, etc... all bonuses are written above the line.

6. All you have to remember is that only game points that are contracted for and made are written under the line. Any other points for any other reason are written above the line.

7. The winner is the one with the most points including all points above and below the line.

♠   ♦

Bridge Tip

The score pad is divided into two columns, one for each team. "We" indicates the team that is keeping the score, with "They" being the other team. The score pad also has a horizontal line dividing the pad into an upper section and lower section. Some of the score is written over that dividing line and some written under the line.

You can see below an example of a bridge score pad.

Score Card

We	They
All other points	
Game points	

Example of Scoring a Simple (2 games to 1) rubber

After 1st hand:
We: Bid 4 Hearts, but made 5 Hearts.
Write game points (4 x 30 =120) under the line,
and points for extra tricks (1 x 30=30) above the line.

We	They
30	
120	

After 2nd hand:

We: Bid 2 Spades, and made it.
Write partial game points (2 x 30 = 60) under the line.
Now "**We**" have "a leg" in the game equal to
60 points.

We	They
30	
120	
60	

Bridge Tip

All you have to remember about writing the score is that only game points that are contracted for, and made, are written under the line. Any other points for any other reason are written above the line. The winner is the one with the most points including all points above and below the line.

After 3rd hand:

They: Bid 2 Clubs, and made it.
Write partial game points (2 x 20 = 40) under the line.
Now "**They**" have "a leg" in the game equal to 40
points.

We	They
30	
120	
60	40

After 4th hand:

They: Bid 2 Hearts, and made it.
Write the score (2 x 30 = 60) under the line.
"**They**" have a game now. Draw a line across the pad.
The 60 point leg that "**We**" had is now cut off, and will
no longer count toward partial game points. However,
the points still counts toward your overall score.

We	They
30	
120	
60	40
	60

After 5th hand:

We: Bid 5 Clubs, and made it.

Write game points (5 x 20 =100) under the line.

Write 500 bonus points for winning the rubber (2 games to 1), above the line. (Bonus points for winning the rubber 2 games to 0 is 700 points).

Total the points, 810 for **We**, and 100 for **They**.

We: won by 710 points. Approx. 700 points.

If you change partners every rubber, and want to know the winner at the end of the game, you divide the points by 100, so you give each in "**We**" +7 points, and each player in "**They**" -7 points. You do the same every rubber and at the end of the match add up the score for each player and find out the winners.

We	They
500	
30	
120	
60	40
	60
100	
810	100

Doubles, Downs, and Bonus Points:

- Any team can challenge the bid of the other team by saying "Double", and sometimes they get a "Re-double" in return. Double means if you make your bid your points will be doubled. If you lose your bid, for every trick you go down, your opponents will gain two times or more the points they would normally get. If you say re-double after your opponents have doubled your bid, it will mean that you will gain or lose even more points depending on the outcome of the hand.

- When you have won a game you are "Vulnerable". Now the points your opponents receive when you do not make your bid are higher. Also, any overtricks you make will be worth more and your slam bonuses will give you more points.

You can refer to the tables on the next few pages for penalties and bonuses when doubled or re-doubled, and for vulnerable or not vulnerable.

Bridge Tip

Double means if you make your bid your points will be doubled. If you lose your bid, for every trick you go down, your opponents will gain two times or more the points they would normally get. If you say re-double after your opponents have doubled your bid, it will mean that you will gain or lose even more points depending on the outcome of the hand.

Table 6: Downs Value*

Downs	Not Vulnerable			Vulnerable		
	Un-doubled	Doubled	Re-Doubled	Un-doubled	Doubled	Re-Doubled
1	50	100	200	100	200	400
2	100	300	600	200	500	1000
3	150	500	1000	300	800	1600
4	200	800	1600	400	1100	2200
5	250	1100	2200	500	1400	2800
6	300	1400	2800	600	1700	3400
7	350	1700	3400	700	2000	4000
8	400	2000	4000	800	2300	4600
9	450	2300	4600	900	2600	5200
10	500	2600	5200	1000	2900	5800
11	550	2900	5800	1100	3200	6400
12	600	3200	6400	1200	3500	7000
13	650	3500	7000	1300	3800	7600

Table 7: Tricks Value

Tricks	Not Vulnerable			Vulnerable		
	Un-doubled	Doubled	Re-Doubled	Un-doubled	Doubled	Re-Doubled
Club	20	40	80	20	40	80
Diamond	20	40	80	20	40	80
Heart	30	60	120	30	60	120
Spade	30	60	120	30	60	120
1st No Trump	40	80	160	40	80	160
No Trump	30	60	120	30	60	120
Over Tricks	Trick value	100	200	Trick value	200	400
Bonus for making a doubled contract: 50						

* Downs are the losing tricks below your bid.

Bridge Tip

When you have won a game, you are "Vulnerable". Now the points your opponents receive when you do not make your bid are higher. Also, any overtricks you make will be worth more, and your slam bonuses will give you more points.

♣   ♥

Table 8: Bonus Points

Plays	Bonus
Rubber 2-0 game	700
Rubber 2-1 game	500
Unfinished rubber (1 game)	300
Partial game score	50
4 honors, A K Q J in one suit*	100
5 honors, A K Q J 10 in one suit*	150
4 Aces when playing No Trump	150

* When playing that suit

Table 9: Slam Bonus

Slam - Bid and Made	Not Vulnerable	Vulnerable
Small slam (12 tricks)	500	750
Grand slam (13 tricks)	1000	1500

Test yourself

Questions:

1. On the score pad, what's written above the line and what's written below the line?

2. How many bonus points do you receive when you win the rubber 2 games to 0, and when you win 2 games to 1?

3. What's the value of 3 No Trumps doubled?

4. What's the grand slam bonus when vulnerable?

Answers:

1. All bonus points are above the line, and all contracted game points are below the line.

2. 750, and 500.

3. 200 points.

4. 1500 points.

Playing Step 7

- In **step 7** we'll practice writing the score. Every player picks a Bridge scoring pad. If you don't have the pre-printed pads, use any paper pad. Divide the paper into 2 columns and draw a line across as shown in the example at the beginning of the chapter.

- Let's assume that Sam and Jane are "**We**" and Alex and Julia are "**They**". The rubber was played as follows:

Practice Scoring:
Table 10: Scoring Practice "No Number"

The Hand	We	They
1st hand	Bid and made 3 NT	
2nd hand		Bid and made 2 clubs
3rd hand	Bid 2 Hearts, and made 4	
4th hand		Bid and made 3 Diamonds
5th hand	Bid 4 Spades, made 3	Bonus for one down: 100
6th hand		Bid and made 4 Hearts, had 4 honors in opening hand

- Write the score for the 1st hand, then the second, third, fourth, fifth, and the six.

- Add up the bonus points for the rubber and total up the points.

- Find out the + and − final points for each player.

- Double check your figures and see if you came up with the same result as in the table below.

- Check your work step by a step against the score card.

We	They
	500
	100
60	100
100	
60	40
	60
90	120
310	920

"They" won by approximately 600 points which is 6 points in the score tally (you divide by 100).

We	They
-6	+6

Name	1st rubber
Sam	-6
Jane	-6
Alex	+6
Julia	+6

STEP 8
MAKING YOUR BID

What you need to know:

1. When you are the Declarer and playing the hand, your goal is to win the most number of tricks possible. The goal is the same for both offense and defense.

2. It's great to make your bid, but it's even better to go over and score extra points.

3. The secret of making your bid is to bid correctly in the first place.

4. Every trick matters and every card matters. You must keep your focus on playing the hand from the first trick to the last trick.

5. You learn a lot by paying attention to your opponent's bid. It will give you clues about the missing honors.

6. When you play the hand, you are either playing a trump contract or no trump contract. They are very different.

In Step 8 you'll learn how to play the hand and maximize your winning tricks. Your team has won the contract and you are the Declarer. You know how many tricks you need to win to make your contract. You also know how many tricks you can afford to lose without going down. Your opponent on your left has led, and your partner opened his cards and laid them down. It's your turn to play from the Dummy, so what should you do?

♠   ♦

Bridge Tip

If you are the Declarer, before you play the first card you should count your winning tricks in the Dummy and your hand combined. Count both the fast tricks and the tricks that you should get. The fast tricks are the tricks that you should win in the first two rounds of play, especially the no strings attached winners like having aces in a no trump hand.

Before you play the first card you should count your winning tricks as you see them in the Dummy and your hand combined. Count both the fast tricks and the tricks that you should get. The fast tricks are the tricks that you should win in the first two rounds of play, especially the no strings attached winners like having aces in a no trump hand. Other winning tricks are the protected honors. For example, if you have the King and the Queen of a suit but your opponents have the Ace. You can't be sure both your King and Queen will win a trick, but you can be sure that at least one of them will. One of your honors will force your opponent to play the Ace leaving your remaining honor as the top card in that suit and a sure winner.

In general a protected honor is one that during the normal course of play will win a trick. For example, if you have a King with one small card, KX - where the "X" is a zero value card, that is called "King 2nd". In this case you should be able to discard the small card when the Ace is played and win with the King the next time the suit is played. If you have a Queen with two small cards, QXX (that's a "Queen 3rd"), the same logic applies.

You will also win extra trump tricks with low cards if you have more of them than your opponent. This will allow you to use your extra trumps to trump your opponent's cards. Long suit tricks should also be counted among your winning tricks.

Remember, counting your winning tricks does not guarantee you will win them all. How you play the hand, how your opponents play defense and the distribution of the cards can cause you to lose a winning trick, but it's still important to do this analysis before you begin playing the hand.

See if your winning tricks are enough to make your bid. If not, you need to develop extra tricks. You get extra tricks by ruffing or crossruffing, establishing long suits, and finessing missing honors. These strategies will be described later in this chapter.

After the first lead:

1- Count your winning tricks.

2- Check for ruffing or crossruffing.

3- Check for an opportunity to establish long suit.

4- Find out if you need to finesse and in which direction.

5- Check your entries to your hand and the Dummy.

6- Plan your strategy for the whole hand.

7- Play the hand.

1 - Count your winning Tricks:

♠ A X X X
♥ A X X
♣ A X X
♦ A X X

4 Fast tricks

Let's start the process by counting the winning tricks – both the fast tricks, and the tricks that you should get.

The above hand shows you an obvious 4 fast tricks in a no trump contract, the four Aces. Let's see a different hand and try to count the winning tricks.

♠ A K Q J 10
♥ 9 5 3
♣ A Q 2
♦ K 4

8 Winning tricks

5 in Spades, 2 in Clubs and 1 in Diamonds

When playing a NT contract, <u>in Spades</u> you have 5 fast tricks, the four honors plus the 2. The 2 will be a winner, assuming everybody is out of Spades. <u>In Clubs</u> you have 1 fast trick, the Ace and 1 possible trick, the Queen. Hopefully after the Ace wins, you discard the 2 against the King and the Queen becomes a winner. <u>In Diamonds</u>, the King is a possible winner because you can discard the 4 against the Ace and make the King a winner. So, the total fast and possible tricks in the above hand are 8 tricks.

Follow the next exercise to practice counting winning tricks in both your hand and the Dummy's hand combined.

Remember, these examples show the most possible tricks you can make, but good defense by your opponents or bad distribution can make some of these tricks disappear.

Dummy	♠ A K 9 3
	♥ Q 10 9 8
	♣ K 5
	♦ 10 5 3

Declarer	♠ 10 9 5
	♥
	♣ A Q J 10 8 7 6 2
	♦ 8 4

11 winning tricks when playing in Clubs.
2 in Spades, 1 in Hearts, and 8 in Clubs.

Dummy	♠ Q J 5 2
	♥ K Q 9 8 7
	♣
	♦ J 4 3 2

Declarer	♠ A K 10 9 8 3
	♥ 5
	♣ A Q 7 4
	♦ A 9

12 winning tricks when playing in Spades.
6 in Spades, 2 in Hearts, 2 in Clubs and 2 in Diamonds.

♣ ♥

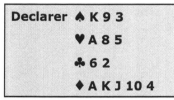

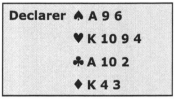

Dummy	♠ J 10 6
	♥ K Q 9 5
	♣ A Q 2
	♦ Q 9 7

Declarer	♠ K 9 3
	♥ A 8 5
	♣ 6 2
	♦ A K J 10 4

Dummy	♠ K J 5 3
	♥ J 8 4
	♣ K Q J 7
	♦ Q 10

Declarer	♠ A 9 6
	♥ K 10 9 4
	♣ A 10 2
	♦ K 4 3

12 winning tricks when playing in Diamonds. 2 in Spades, 3 in Hearts, 2 in Clubs and 5 in Diamonds.

10 winning tricks when playing in NT. 3 in Spades, 2 in Hearts, 4 in Clubs and 2 in Diamonds

2 - Check for ruffing or crossruffing:

Ruffing is trumping that is done on purpose. You play from the Dummy and trump from your hand, or play from your hand and trump from the Dummy. If you can do it both ways at the same time, that's crossruffing, and a great way to increase your trump winning tricks.

If you have a singleton or doubleton in a particular suit, sometimes you want to make yourself void in that suit early on to cash in 1 or 2 rounds of ruffing.

However, don't forget that you still have to collect the trumps from your opponents. When you plan your strategy, decide on when to collect the trumps. When you have strong "control" of the trumps (most of the trump cards and most of the honors in trump) you may want to clear out your opponents trumps right away. However, in the situation described above you may want to delay collecting the trumps until you capture tricks with a couple of rounds of ruffing.

♠   ♦

Bridge Tip

Ruffing is trumping that is done on purpose. You play from the Dummy and trump from your hand, or play from your hand and trump from the Dummy. If you can do it both ways at the same time, that's crossruffing, and a great way to increase your trump winning tricks.

3 - Check for an opportunity to establish long suit:

A long suit is a suit where you or your Dummy have 5 cards or more, headed by at least two honors. In even distribution, 3 rounds of play in any suit will use 12 cards and leave 1 card left which becomes a "master", i.e. a definite winner. If you have 5 cards in a suit your first 4 cards will usually collect the suit and leave you with 1 master. If you have 6 cards you'll end up with 2 masters.

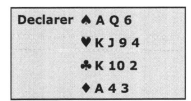

Dummy	♠ J 10
	♥ Q 7 3
	♣ Q J 7
	♦ K J 10 5 2

Declarer	♠ A Q 6
	♥ K J 9 4
	♣ K 10 2
	♦ A 4 3

Bid: 3 NT

When you develop a long suit you are making masters out of small cards. You need to get your honors and your opponents honors out of the way first, so your small cards can become masters.

In the above hand, you decided to play 3 NT instead of 5 Diamonds because it's easier to win 9 tricks in NT, vs. 11 tricks in Diamonds. In order to make your bid, you need to take advantage of your Diamonds by establishing it as a long suit. Your total cards in Diamonds are 8 cards, so there are 5 cards with your

Bridge Tip

A long suit is a suit where you or your Dummy have 5 cards or more, headed by at least two honors. In even distribution, 3 rounds of play in a given suit will use 12 cards and leave 1 card left which becomes a "master", i.e. a definite winner.

♣   ♥

opponents. The most likely possibility is that they will be split 3 and 2. There's a chance that the missing Queen is in the group of two cards and thus not protected by low cards. You should play the Ace and then the King and hope the Queen will drop. If not, let your opponent win the Queen by leading Diamond again. Now after 3 rounds the 5 and 2 of Diamonds are masters.

4 - Find out if you need to finesse and in which direction:

Finesse is a play designed to take away a winner from your opponents. The cards must lie in the right position in order for this to work. Below are two finesse opportunities.

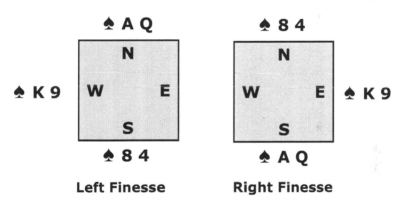

Left Finesse   **Right Finesse**

In the left finesse, the cards are set perfectly to finesse the King on the left. You are "South", the declarer, and your Dummy is "North". It's your lead from your hand, so you lead one of the two small Spades. Your opponent wants to save his King until the Ace is played, so he plays the 9. From the Dummy you finesse the King by playing the Queen instead of the Ace. You will win the trick because the finesse was successful. Then you lead the Ace from the Dummy, and force the King out and win the second trick.

♠   ♦

Bridge Tip

When playing a contract in a trump suit, collect the trumps first as soon as you get the lead. Only in special cases do you delay collecting trumps like in ruffing and crossruffing cases. When playing No Trump, get rid of your losers first so you can cash your winners later without interruptions.

♣ ♥

In the right finesse, you lead from the Dummy and you finesse the King on your right by playing the Queen from your hand. Then you lead the Ace from your hand and force the king out same as in the left finesse above.

Before you decide to finesse, you need to guess where the missing honor is and what direction the cards will allow your finesse, left or right?

If you guess that the player on your left has the King of Spades, and the cards are set for a left finesse as shown on page 119, then you have perfect conditions for a finesse. If the cards are not set for your desired finesse don't do it.

You get clues about the location of the King from your opponent's bids. The one that bid in Spades might have the King of Spades. The one with a stronger hand is more likely to have more honors and more likely to have the King.

You might also get a clue from the first lead. It's unlikely for the opponent with the King of Spades to lead in Spades. He usually saves his Spades to protect his King. You can also get clues from the distribution of the cards by guessing how many cards in each suit each opponent has. The one with more Spades is more likely to have the King.

No matter how well you do your calculations you might lose the finesse. That's why the best time to finesse is when you can afford to lose it. This happens when the finesse is done to get an overtrick or when even a losing finesse will establish one of your other cards as a winner.

5 - Check your entries to your hand and the Dummy:

If you play a card from your hand and the Dummy wins the trick, that's an entry to the Dummy because the next play will be from the Dummy. If you play a card from the Dummy and your hand wins, that's an entry to your hand.

That's what "entries" mean; entering the Dummy to play from the Dummy, or entering your hand to play from your hand. It's essential that you have enough entries to execute your plan and win your fast tricks and your developed tricks. Usually the hand with fewer high cards and fewer trumps is the one to worry about when it comes to entries. At the beginning of the hand evaluate if the entries you think you need are there. Sometimes you have to "develop" an entry. An example could be a situation where you have a King of a suit in your hand and a Queen of a suit in Dummy. You may choose to use your King to force out or lose to your opponents Ace so that you can later win with the Queen and have an entry to Dummy.

Dummy ♠ J 10 6
♥ K Q 9 5
♣ A Q 2
♦ Q 9 7

Possible 5 entries

Dummy ♠ K J 5 3
♥ J 8 4
♣ K Q J 7
♦ Q 10

Possible 7 entries

Declarer ♠ K 9 3
♥ A 8 4
♣ 6 3
♦ A K J 10 4

Possible 6 entries

Declarer ♠ A 9 6
♥ K 10 9 2
♣ A 10 2
♦ K 4 3

Possible 4 entries

Bridge Tip

*Count cards by counting rounds.
If you played 2 rounds of Spades,
and everybody had Spades to play,
then 8 Spades have been played.
Add them to the Spades in your
hand and in your Dummy and
you'll figure out how many Spades
are left with the opponents. You
are constantly counting cards, and
counting rounds throughout the
play of the hand. If you lose your
focus, you lose count and
probably lose the game.*

6 - Plan your strategy for the whole hand:

Example 1: Playing a 5 Clubs Contract:

South is the declarer, and West led the 2 of Diamonds.

The Plan:

The declarer needs to win 11 tricks in Clubs, which means he can only afford to lose 2 tricks. His winning tricks are 5 tricks in Clubs, 2 tricks in Diamonds, 2 tricks in Hearts, and 2 tricks in Spades. If a successful finesse for the King of Spades happens, then it would be 3 tricks in Spades. Declarer knows he can make his contract whether or not his finesse for the King of Spades is successful.

The declarer's general plan will be to collect the trumps from the opponents, then finesse the King of Spades on the left, just to try for an extra trick. He will then cash the rest of his fast tricks.

Usually collecting the trumps first is the right thing to do. The declarer counts the trumps in his hand and the Dummy's hand. They have a total of 8 trumps and there are 5 trumps which the opponents have. The Declarer can collect these trumps in three rounds or more, depending on how the 5 trumps will break. The odds are the trumps will break 3-2.

7 - Play The Hand:

When collecting the trumps, the declarer wants his hand to win the last round so he can lead again from his hand to try the left finesse. Now the plan is all done, West had led the ♦**2**. The declarer can play the first card from the Dummy. In this case the ♦**8**, East will play the ♦**A**, and South will discard the ♦**Q**.

♣ ♥

Example 1:

♠ A Q 4
♥ K 9 3
♣ K 6 3
♦ J 8 6 5

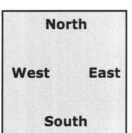

♠ K 10 3		♠ 8 6 5 2
♥ Q 5 2	North	♥ J 8 6 4
♣ 10 7 4	West East	♣ 8 5
♦ 9 7 4 2	South	♦ A 10 3

♠ J 9 7
♥ A 10 7
♣ A Q J 9 2
♦ K Q

South (Dealer)	West	North	East
18 points	5 points	13 points	6 points
5 card suit	No suit	3 Trumps	No suit
1 Club	Pass	3 Clubs	Pass
5 Clubs	Pass	Pass	Pass

Playing a 5 Clubs Contract
South is the Declarer, and West led the 2 of Diamonds.

♠   ♦   125

East wins the trick and plays Diamonds again. South wins the trick with the King of Diamonds and starts executing his plan. South will lead small Club from his hand and wins with the King from the Dummy. Then South leads a small Club from the Dummy and wins with the ♣A from his hand. So far 2 rounds have been played in trumps. He leads the ♣Q from his hand, and wins the third round. He knows by counting that his opponents are out of trump.

After all the trumps are out, the declarer will attempt his left finesse by leading the Jack of Spades from his hand. If West follows one of the defensive tips presented in the next chapter ("cover an honor with an honor") he may eventually take a Spade trick with his 10. If West plays a small card, declarer will play a small card from the Dummy as well. Now East will also play a small card because he doesn't have any card higher than the Jack.

Declarer now knows that his finesse was successful, and the King of Spades is with West. Declarer will now lead a small Spade from his hand. West will play the ♠10, and the Dummy will win with the ♠Q. In the next round the King of Spades will drop against the Ace of Spades.

Re-Capping:

The declarer is always counting the cards and the rounds. By now 2 rounds of Diamonds have been played, 5 Diamond cards are left, 3 rounds of trumps have been played, and only 2 trumps are left in the declarer's hand. Also 3 rounds of Spades have been played and 1 Spade is left in the opponents' hands. Now the declarer has won 7 tricks. He won book, plus 1, which means 1 Club, and still has to win 4 more tricks to make his contract.

Playing The Hand Continues:

The Dummy won the last trick played. So, the declarer leads the ♦J from the Dummy. The declarer discards the ♥7. Dummy wins the trick and leads again. He plays the ♥K and wins it, and leads the ♥3 from the Dummy, and wins it from his hand with the ♥A.

Re-Capping:

Now the declarer has added 3 more tricks to his winnings, make it 4 Clubs so far, and still has to win one more trick to make his contract. Since he has 2 cards left in his hand, and they are both trumps, both are sure winners.

Playing The Hand Continues:

The declarer plays the remaining 2 trump cards and wins them both. Now, he made 12 tricks in Clubs, his contract plus 1 extra trick.

Example 2:
Playing a 3 No Trump Contract

South is the Declarer, and West led the 2 of Hearts.

The Plan:

The declarer needs to win 9 tricks to make his contract, which means he can lose 4 tricks without going down. He has 2 tricks in Spades, 2 in Hearts, 3 in Clubs, and 2 in Diamonds. That's a total of 9 tricks and that's all the declarer needs to make his contract. When playing NT, it's better to get the losers out of your way and then you cash your winners without interruption.

The declarer wants to force the Ace of Diamonds out so he can make the King and the Queen of Diamonds masters. He also wants to finesse the Queen of Clubs and secure the rest of the Clubs as winners. That will be 2 tricks in Diamonds and with a successful finesse, 4 tricks in Clubs. 2 sure tricks in Hearts because of the lead in Hearts, and 1 sure trick in Spades for a total of 9 tricks.

If the finesse was not successful, then one more trick is needed. It could be from Spades or Hearts.

Playing The Hand:

West had led ♥2, the declarer plays the ♥3 from the Dummy. East plays the ♥8 and the declarer wins the trick with ♥10. He plays the ♥7 from his hand and West wins the trick with the King then leads the ♥5. The declarer wins it with the ♥A and leads the ♦5. East wins the trick with the ♦A and leads the ♠2. South plays ♠10, and west the ♠K. Then the Dummy wins with the ♠A and leads the ♦8.

Example 2:

♠ A 8 4
♥ Q 9 3
♣ K 6 3 2
♦ J 8 6

♠ K 7 3   **North**   ♠ J 6 5 2
♥ K J 5 2   ♥ 8 6 4
♣ Q 7 4   **West   East**   ♣ 8 5
♦ 9 7 4   ♦ A 10 3 2
                   South

♠ Q 10 9
♥ A 10 7
♣ A J 10 9
♦ K Q 5

South (Dir)	West	North	East
16 points	9 points	10 points	6 points
Balanced Distribution	No suit	Balanced Distribution	No suit
1 NT	Pass	2 NT	Pass
3 NT	Pass	Pass	Pass

Playing a 3 No Trumps Contract:
South is the declarer, and West led the 2 of Hearts.

♠   ♦   129

Re-Capping:

So far, the declarer won 2 tricks in Hearts and 1 in Spades. The opponents won 2 tricks, one in Hearts and one in Diamonds, and they should not win more than 2 more tricks. The declarer should win 2 quick tricks in Diamonds. He can also make 4 more tricks in Clubs with a successful left finesse. Or, if he misses the finesse, he still can win 3 tricks in Clubs and add 1 trick in Spades by the ♠Q, and make his contract.

Playing The Hand Continues:

After ♦**8** is led from the Dummy, the declarer wins this trick with the ♦**K** and leads the ♦**Q**, and wins again. Now it's time to attempt the finesse.

The declarer leads ♣**J** from his hand, West plays ♣**4**, the Dummy ♣**2**, and East plays the ♣**5**. The finesse was successful and the declarer won the trick. Now he knows the ♣**Q** is with West and he repeats the same play by leading ♣**10**. West will play ♣**7**, the Dummy plays ♣**3**, and East plays ♣**8**. Now the declarer is 2 away from his contract but he has 3 sure winners, ♣**A**, ♣**K**, and ♠**Q**.

The declarer plays ♣**A**, forcing the ♣**Q** out, and wins the trick. Then he leads ♣**9** and wins the trick from the Dummy with the ♣**K**. The Dummy leads ♠**4**, East plays ♠**6**. At this point the declarer has already made his contract. He can afford to risk another finesse by finessing the Jack of Spades on the right. He plays the ♠9 instead of the ♠**Q** and finesses the Jack. West plays ♠**3**, the declarer wins, and the finesse is successful. Now the declarer plays the ♠**Q** and wins the last trick. The declarer won his contract and made two over tricks. The defenders won only 2 tricks.

Test yourself

Questions:

1. What are the entries?

2. What is ruffing, and crossruffing?

3. If you are finessing the King, where should the Ace be in each case?

   (A) Left finesse. (B) Right finesse.

4. What is the first thing the declarer should do before playing the first card?

Answers:

1. Entries are cards that enable you to go from your hand to the Dummy and vice versa so you can lead a card from your desired spot.

2. Ruffing is trumping that is done on purpose. You play from the Dummy and trump from your hand, or play from your hand and trump from the Dummy. If you can do it both ways at the same time, that's crossruffing.

3. (A) At the Dummy. (B) At your hand.

4. Count his winning tricks.

Playing Step 8

- Playing the hand is the most exciting part of the Bridge game.

- You have been playing the hand since the first step but now will add more tools to help you make your bid.

- Distribute the cards and start the bidding like before until there's a declarer. The player on the left of the declarer leads and the Dummy opens his hand and lays them down starting from the trump on the left and alternate colors after that with the highest rank first. In case of NT, start with Spades since Spade is the highest ranked suit.

- Now the declarer will take a moment, and make a plan for playing this hand by following these easy steps:

  1. Find out how many tricks you need to win and how many tricks you can lose without going down.

  2. Count your winning tricks and see if they are enough to make your contract. If not, then you need to develop extra tricks.

  3. You can develop extra tricks from trumping, leveraging long suits, and finessing missing honors.

  4. Plan your entries to the Dummy and to your hand, right from the start. Always know your next play before playing the current trick.

  5. When playing a contract in a trump suit, collect the trump first as soon as you get the lead. Only in special cases do you delay collecting the trumps like in ruffing and crossruffing.

6. When playing no trump, get rid of your losers first so you can cash your winners without interruptions.

Additional Tips

- Keep your focus while playing the hand. Don't drink, eat, or engage in conversation until you are all done.

- Count cards by counting rounds. If you played 2 rounds of Spades, and everybody had Spades to play, then 8 Spades are played. Add them to the Spades in your hand and in your Dummy and you'll figure out how many Spades are left with the opponents.

- You are constantly counting cards and counting rounds throughout the play of the hand. If you lose your focus, you lose count and you may lose the game.

- It will help you count if you play one suit at a time until the suit is concluded. Always watch your entries when you do that, and make sure you have enough entries to make your contract.

- In closing, the secret of playing a great hand of Bridge is to plan your tricks in advance. Practice planning 1 or 2 tricks in advance, then 3 or 4 tricks in advance. Later you'll find yourself comfortable planning the whole hand in advance.

- At the end of step 8, count your tricks and see if you made your contract.

STEP 9
PLAYING DEFENSE

What you need to know:

1. If you want to be effective in defending, you have to keep your focus, count the cards and count the rounds just like the declarer.

2. The declarer has an advantage over you because he can play from two hands, the Dummy and his hand. He can also see both hands at the same time and in most instances has the best cards.

3. The Defenders can't see each other hands, but they can communicate through bidding and through the cards they play.

4. A defender needs to pay attention to the opponent's bid because what the opponents don't have, his partner might have.

5. Often times the most difficult play in the bridge game is the opening lead. The defender on the left of the declarer is the one to do it.

6. There are a few basic defensive strategies that will help you defeat your opponents. However, there are no defensive "rules of play". You must evaluate each hand and each play on a case by case basis to see if applying one of these strategies makes sense.

In Step 9, you'll learn about playing defense. It's not as glamorous as playing the hand but it requires a lot of skill and can be exciting. Remember, in bridge you will be playing defense about half the time. Often times beginners feel that the only "fun" part of bridge is playing a hand. However, knowing just a few basic things about playing defense can improve your enjoyment of the game immensely.

Playing defense actually starts with the bidding. After just the first round of bidding you often will know who has the strongest hand, who will be playing the hand and who will be defending.

Bidding as a Defensive Strategy:

1. Make a bid if you can during the bidding round. It will at least help your partner know your strength.

2. At the end of the bidding, double if you think you can set the opponents.

3. Don't double if your double will give your opponents a game. For example don't double 2 Spades, because 2 Spades doubled are 120 points and enough for a game. 2 Spades undoubled is 60 points and only a partial game.

4. If you have 6-10 points, and 7 card suit (or more) you can make a pre-emptive bid to prevent your opponents from communicating effectively with each other and finding a bid that they could make.

Opening Lead:

The opening lead can many times make or break a contract. A good opening lead can help set the opponents, while a bad opening lead can help them make their contract and maybe even lead to overtricks.

Once the opening lead is played, the Dummy will open his hand and the defenders will be able to see how the strength of the opponents is distributed.

The bidding is finished and you have the opening lead. The first thing to do before leading is to remember how the bidding went. The common wisdom in choosing a suit regardless if you are playing no trump or trump suit, is to consider your partner's bid suit first. Play in your partner's bid suit, or play in the suit that your partner doubled.

What if your partner didn't bid? If you have a strong suit lead that. (See the charts on pages 141 and 142 for hints on which card in your strong suit you should lead.) This is especially important in a no trump hand. In no trump you need to attack the declarer's weakest suit as soon as possible. Your best suit may be declarer's weakest.

What if your partner didn't bid and you don't have a particularly good suit to lead? Again, listen to the bidding. Was there a suit that neither declarer nor Dummy bid? If your opponents ended up bidding three suits, there is a strong possibility that the unbid suit will be your partner's strongest. Lead that suit.

Bridge Tip

The opening lead can many times make or break a contract. You can summarize the preference in picking the opening suit in the following order:

1. Play in your partner's strength.

2. Play in your own strength.

3. Play in the un-bid suit.

4. Play in the Dummy's strength.

5. Play in the trump suit.

♣   ♥

A common bidding sequence is as follows: your opponent bids one of something, you pass, your opponent's partner bids another suit, your partner passes, the first bidder rebids his opening suit, you pass and your opponent's partner either passes or bids his partner's suit. At the end of the bidding sequence your partner has not bid and there are two unbid suits. If you don't have a strong suit lead the suit that Dummy bid. Why would you do this? If your partner has some strength in this suit you may successfully run a finesse right through Dummy. This may allow your partner to win a trick right away or set up a future trick.

Leading a trump is generally not a good idea as it may finesse a possible winning trump trick away from your partner. However, when you're pretty sure that your opponents have all of the top trumps and want to deplete the declarer's trumps to limit his ability to ruff, leading a trump can be an effective lead. It is recommended that you get a little more experience playing bridge before you consider this opening lead.

Sometimes your "weakest" suit can be your "strongest" in terms of making an opening lead. If you lead a singleton that your partner can win, he can lead that suit back to you for a ruffing trick. If you have a singleton, don't consider this an automatic best lead. Leading a singleton trump for example, is probably not a good lead most of the time, so you need to do the same evaluation of the bidding process before making your lead.

You can summarize the preference in picking the opening suit in the following order:

1. Play in your partner's strength.
2. Play in your own strength.
3. Play in the un-bid suit.
4. Play in the Dummy's strength.
5. Play in the trump suit.

In summary, if your partner didn't bid, play in your best suit. In no trump contract, play your best longest suit. If neither your partner nor you have a suit to play in, then play in the un-bid suit. Your partner might have strength in the un-bid suit. The last choice is to play in the Dummy's bid suit that declarer didn't answer. Maybe your partner has some strength in that.

Don't play to the declarer's strength unless you are playing a trump card and you want to deplete the declarer's trumps. Sometimes when you don't have a good lead and you're pretty sure declarer has all the high trumps, playing in the trump suit is your next best thing.

Now that you know which suit you should lead with, check the Lead Card table on the next page to learn which card is the best card to lead with in a suit contract.

Table 11: Lead Card – Suit Contract

Condition	Cards	Suit	Lead
If your partner made a bid, lead in your partner's suit. If you have two honors in your partner's suit, play the highest. If you have 1 honor, play the lowest card except if the honor is the Ace. Always play the Ace.	If you have an Ace in your partner's suit.	AXX	Ace
	2 card suit, or 2 card sequence, play the highest	J10	J
	3 card sequence, play the highest	KQJ	K
	3 card suit headed by 2 honors, play the highest	QJX	Q
	4 card suit headed by 2 honors, play the highest	KQXX	K
	1 honor in a 3 or 4 card suit, play the lowest.	KXX	X
If your partner has not made a bid. The rule still applies. If you have two honors in a suit, play the highest. If you have 1 honor, play the lowest card. In this case you don't always play the Ace. If you have AQX, don't play the Ace. You might win 2 tricks if you wait.	2 card suit, or 2 card sequence, play the highest	AK	Ace
	3 card sequence, play the highest	KQJ	K
	1 honor in a 3 or 4 card suit, play the lowest.	KXX	X
	Ace, Queen sequence	AQX	Do not lead this suit

♠　　♦　　　　　　　　　　　　　　　　141

Check the table below for best card to lead in no trump contract.

Table 12: Lead Card – NT Contract

Condition	Cards	Suit	Lead
If your partner has not made a bid. Lead your own suit. If you don't have a suit, lead in the Dummy's bid suit that declarer didn't respond to.	Lead the 4th highest from your longest suit	QJ9732	7
	Lead the lowest from 3 or 4 card suit.	Q105	5
	Lead the highest from 2 card suit.	J9	J

STRATEGIES OF PLAY

Two Defenders, One Declarer:

If it sounds like two against one, it is. Your opponents may have the best cards but you have the advantage of working together as a team if you communicate well with each other.

Good communication:

Good communication starts at the bidding round. You should always remember your partner's bid. This will give you an idea of what your partner's hand looks like. If your partner has bid a suit it is generally a good suit to lead back to him when you have the opportunity. The opening lead is a great tool of communication. Look at the five options given for an opening lead and figure out what your partner is saying about his hand.

You can also watch for communication opportunities during the play of the hand. When you lead a suit, unless it's a lead to your partner's strong suit, it communicates to your partner that when he has the opportunity he should lead that suit back to you.

High-Low Signal:

A more subtle communication mechanism is the high-low signal. If you lead a suit, it's easy for your partner to know what suit to return to you. But, if your partner leads a suit and you're not able to take that trick, how can you tell him to play it again because you have a winner in that suit? The basic high-low communication strategy is this: If you like the suit your partner led and want him to lead it back to you, play a high card. If you don't like the suit, play a low card. A "high" card would be an eight, nine, or even a ten, but not a card you think may win a future trick.

For example, if you have ♠Q952, the first time your partner plays Spade, you play high, ♠9. That should signal your partner to play Spade again. If you didn't have the Queen of Spades play the two.

Avoiding Finessing each other:

A finesse is an attempt to take away a winner from your opponents by setting up or making sure that one of your team's cards will win a trick that you might otherwise lose (see step 8).

Think of the table as a finesse playing ground. Avoid making a play that will finesse your partner's honors, and always try to make a play that will finesse the Dummy or the declarer.

You are "West", and have ♠**985**, while the Dummy has ♠**AQ10.** You play a Spade. The King of Spades might be with your partner and you have just made it a sure winner. The declarer will have to choose between the Ace, or the Queen. If he played the Ace, your partner will win with the King the next time a Spade is played. If the declarer plays the Queen, your partner will win with his King now and, after the Ace is played, he can win again with the Jack.

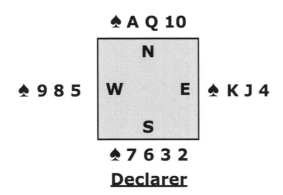

Here's another situation where you are "West", and
you have the lead. After a quick look at the Dummy's
Hearts, it's obvious that the strength in Hearts is
distributed between "East", and the declarer. In that
situation you shouldn't lead in Hearts. If you lead in
Hearts, you will be finessing your partner.

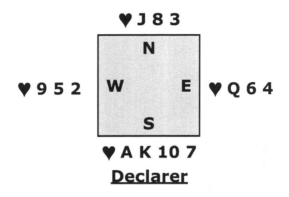

♥ J 8 3

♥ 9 5 2   W   E   ♥ Q 6 4

♥ A K 10 7
<u>Declarer</u>

Bridge Tip

A finesse is an attempt to take away a winner from your opponents. While playing defense, think of the table as a finesse playing ground. Avoid making a play that will finesse your partner, and always try to make a play that will finesse the Dummy or the declarer.

Other Strategies:

There are a number of strategies in playing defense that are often expressed as rules. The following are three of them. Please think of them as suggested strategies and not as rules. Bridge is a game where you always need to look at each play on a case by case basis and only make the play when it makes sense.

• Second Hand Low

If you are the second person to play after the declarer leads a card, it is often a good idea to play a low card. Why is that? The chances are your opponent doesn't know for sure where all the high cards in this suit are. If you play a low card he will need to play a high card from the Dummy to make sure that your partner doesn't win an easy trick with a slightly higher card.

• Third Hand High

If you are the third person to play and no high cards have been played, it is often a good idea to play a high card. Why is that? In the first place you may actually win the trick. But even if you don't, you don't want your opponents to take what is called a "cheap trick". You must force your opponent to win with a high card instead of a low card that is only slightly higher than the cards that have been played.

Bridge Tip

A more subtle communication mechanism is the high-low signal. If you like the suit your partner led and want him to lead it back to you, play a high card. If you don't like the suit play a low card. A "high" card can be an eight, nine or even a ten, but not a card you think may win a future trick.

• Cover an Honor with an Honor

If the declarer (either from his hand or the board) plays an honor and you have the next play, it is often a good idea to play an honor that is higher than the card the Declarer played. That's why they call it "cover an honor with an honor." Why is that? In order for your opponents to win this trick, they will have to play another honor higher than yours. Thus they had to use two high cards to take one of yours possibly setting up a trick for you later on in the hand.

In summary, to play good defense you must most importantly pay attention to what your opponents and partner bid and what information is coming from their play. Communicate with your partner. If your partner leads a suit he most likely wants it led back to him. Take advantage of the high-low communications strategy. Remember a few strategic suggestions, finesse your opponents, play second hand low, third hand high and cover an honor with an honor. Remember that bridge is a thinking game and apply these strategies only when the play makes sense. If you do all that, you'll be playing good defense.

Test yourself

Questions:

1. What's considered the most difficult play in the Bridge game?
2. What is the preference in picking the opening suit, (A) play in your partner's strength, or (B) play in your own strength?
3. If you have the Ace and the Jack in your partner's suit, which card do you lead?
4. If you have a sequence of honors, which one to lead?
5. What's the high-low signal?

Answers:

1. The opening lead.
2. Play in your partner's strength.
3. The Ace.
4. The highest.
5. If you like the suit your partner led and want him to lead it back to you, play a high card. If you don't like the suit, play a low card.

Playing Step 9

- In **step 9**, you play the hand just like before, only this time you will learn extra tips about good defense.

- After the bidding round, the 1st defensive play is the opening lead. When you choose the opening lead, do it in two steps. First choose the opening suit, then choose the card from that suit.

- Leading with the Ace is only good when you have a good strategic reason for doing so. Otherwise, you will be helping your opponents make their King and other lower cards "winners" for a cheap.

- Your first choice for an opening suit should be your partner's best suit, then your best suit, then the un-bid suit, and last the Dummy's bid suit.

- If you have 2 or more honors in the opening suit, play the highest. If you have 1 honor in a 3 card suit, play the smallest card unless that honor is the Ace, in which case play the Ace. Never lead from AQX suit because you could win both the Ace and the Queen if somebody else led that suit.

- In no trump, lead your 4th best card in your best suit. When choosing your best suit, choose your strongest and longest suit.

- Please refer to the opening lead tables 11 and 12 on pages 141 and 142 for more details.

- In a round of cards, if you are the 2nd to play, play low. If you are the 3rd to play, play high. Cover an honor with an honor. Those tips are guidelines and should be only used on a case by case basis.

- Avoid making a play that will finesse your partner's honors and always try to make a play that will finesse the Dummy or the declarer.

- Remember it's often a good idea to return your partner's played suit. If you have previously led a suit, remember if your partner gave you a high or a low signal. If high, play that suit again. If low, look for something else.

STEP 10
BIDDING FOR A SLAM

What you need to know:

- Bidding and scoring 6 in NT or any other suit is a small slam. That's a contract to win 12 tricks, which are all the tricks in the hand except one. Bidding and scoring 7 is a grand slam. That's a contract to win 13 tricks, which are all the tricks in the hand.

- You receive 500 points bonus for scoring a small slam and 1000 for a grand slam. If you are vulnerable you receive 750 points for a small slam and 1500 points for a grand slam. Making 12 or 13 tricks without bidding for a slam is not considered a slam and doesn't receive bonus points.

- You bid for a slam when you have enough points. It usually takes 33 points to score a small slam and 37 points to score a grand slam.

- There are conventions you can use in bidding for a slam. The Blackwood Convention is a way of asking your partner for the number of Aces and Kings he has starting at 4 No Trumps. The Gerber Convention does the same thing but it starts at 4 Clubs. These conventions are very important when playing a slam in a suit. If you are playing a slam in NT there is no need to ask your partner for his Aces or Kings. You can rely solely on the point count.

In Step 10 you will learn how to bid a slam. Playing a slam is the most exciting part of Bridge playing. How you play a slam is no different than the techniques of play covered in Step 8. The key is knowing how to get to slam through the bidding process.

Bridge Tip

Bidding and scoring 6 in NT or any other suit is a small slam. That's a contract to win 12 tricks, which are all the tricks in the hand except one. Bidding and scoring 7 is a grand slam. That's a contract to win 13 tricks, which are all the tricks in the hand.

♣ ♥

Bidding No Trump Slam:

Bidding a no trump slam is the easiest slam bid. The bidding is based solely on the number of honor points you and your partner have together. Remember, there are 40 honor points in the deck. If your partner opened 2 NT, and you have 11 points in your hand, you can respond 6 NT. A 2 NT opening is 22 points minimum and you have 11 points. That's a total of 33 points, which is enough for a small slam. Why do you need at least 33 points? Because if you and your partner have 33 points your opponents can't have more than one ace, with aces being the only sure winners for your opponents in no trump. If you had 15 points you can go to 7 NT because your total points are minimum 37. Why 37 points? The same logic applies. When your partnership has 37 points your opponents can't have an Ace.

To bid for a NT slam, you only need balanced distribution just like anytime you play NT. What helps you the most is the correct opening bid in the first place. If your partner under bid by opening 1 NT instead of 2 NT, your team might miss a slam opportunity. When openers and responders underbid they end up missing a lot of slams.

When you open in NT it should be clear to you how many points you need to have. You need a minimum of 16 points to open 1 NT and a minimum of 22 points to open 2 NT. So if your partner opens in NT, it's your responsibility to add up your team's total points and come up with the correct response. You are the one who will stop at 3 NT, or go to 6 or 7 NT depending on the total points.

Bridge Tip

You receive 500 points bonus for scoring a small slam, and 1000 for a grand slam. If you are vulnerable you receive 750 points for a small slam and 1500 points for a grand slam. Making 12 or 13 tricks without bidding for a slam is not considered a slam and doesn't receive bonus points.

Bidding Suit Slam:

Bidding slam in a suit is different than NT. When you bid NT you only count the honor points and not the distribution points, but when you bid in a suit you count everything. This will make it tricky, because 33 or 37 points could be missing crucial honors.

That's why you have to know how many Aces there are in your partner's hand, and sometimes how many Kings, before you go to slam. If your partner doesn't have at least one of the two missing Aces, maybe you should stay at 5 and not go to slam.

There are two conventions you can use to ask for Aces or Kings, the Blackwood Convention and the Gerber Convention.

The Blackwood Convention:

An opening of 1 Spade indicates a 13 to 21 point hand. If your partner responds 3 Spades it shows 13-15 points. If your opening bid of 1 Spade was on the high side you are in the slam zone. This is the time to use the Blackwood Convention to ask your partner how many Aces he has and to later ask the same question about his Kings.

Ask for Aces by jumping to 4 NT:
Your partner will respond as follows:

No Aces: 5 Clubs
One Ace: 5 Diamonds
Two Aces: 5 Hearts
Three Aces: 5 Spades
Four Aces: 5 Clubs

♠   ♦

In spite of the fact that 5 Clubs has two meanings, either no Aces or all Aces, it is easy to distinguish the difference. The 5 Clubs response in almost all cases means no Aces. If you ask for Aces while having none, 5 Clubs will definitely mean 4 Aces.

Ask for Kings by bidding 5 NT:
Your partner will respond as follows:

No Kings: 6 Clubs
One King: 6 Diamonds
Two Kings: 6 Hearts
Three Kings: 6 Spades
Four Kings: 6 Clubs

This bid is the same as asking for Aces. You can always tell if your partner means no Kings or 4 Kings.

The Gerber Convention:

One drawback to the Blackwood Convention is that your response starts at the five level immediately. If your partner doesn't have what you hoped, you don't have much room to maneuver to find your best bid. That's why some players prefer to use the Gerber Convention which also asks for Aces and Kings but the response starts at the four level instead of the five.

Ask for Aces by jumping to 4 Clubs:
Your partner will respond as follows:

No Aces: 4 Diamonds
One Ace: 4 Hearts
Two Aces: 4 Spades
Three Aces: 4 NT
Four Aces: 4 Diamonds

Ask for Kings by bidding 5 Clubs:
Your partner will respond as follows:

No Kings: 5 Diamonds
One King: 5 Hearts
Two Kings: 5 Spades
Three Kings: 5 NT
Four Kings: 5 Diamonds

Using the previous example, if you opened 1 Spade and your partner responded with 3 Spades. You need to count up your combined points to see if you are in the slam zone. If you decide to try and go for slam, using the Gerber Convention you would then bid 4 Clubs.

Before using the Blackwood or Gerber Convention you and your partner need to discuss and agree on what convention you intend to use before you start that evening's play. Your opponents need to be aware of that choice as well.

Bridge Tip

You can use the Blackwood Convention to ask your partner for his Aces and Kings by jumping to 4 NT, or use the Gerber Convention by jumping to 4 Clubs. These conventions are very important when playing a slam in a suit. If you are playing a slam in NT there is no need to ask your partner for his Aces or Kings. You can rely solely on the point count.

Below are some slam bids exercises:

♠ A Q 4
♥ K 9 3
♣ K J 6
♦ A 10 6 5

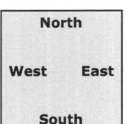

♠ K 10 3
♥ 10 5 2
♣ 10 7 4
♦ 9 7 4 2

♠ 8 6 5 2
♥ Q 8 6 4
♣ 8 5 2
♦ J 8

♠ J 9 7
♥ A J 7
♣ A Q 9 3
♦ K Q 3

South (D)	West	North	East
1 NT	Pass	6 NT	Pass
Pass	Pass		

Example 1:

In example 1, the bidding was "cut and dry". The dealer opened 1 NT, which means minimum 16 honor points. North with 17 honor points did the math, and figured out that their team has 33 points or more. North responded 6 NT. Everybody passed. West leads the ♠3, South will finesse ♠K by playing ♠4 from the Dummy, and winning the trick with the ♠J. If successful he'll play Spades again until the King is dropped. If West didn't lead in Spades, declarer should attempt the finesse any way. The declarer will win 4 tricks in Diamonds, 4 tricks in Clubs, 2 tricks in Hearts, and 2 or 3 tricks in Spades depending on the result of the finesse. So, declarer will make 6 NT for sure and maybe 7 with a successful finesse.

Example 2:

♠ K Q 8 4
♥ K 9
♣ K J 6 2
♦ A J 6

♠ 3		♠ 6 5
♥ J 5 3 2	**North**	♥ Q 8 6 4
♣ Q 7 4 3	**West East**	♣ 9 8 5
♦ 9 7 5 4	**South**	♦ 10 8 3 2

♠ A J 10 9 7 2
♥ A 10 7
♣ A 10
♦ K Q

South (D)	West	North	East
1 Spade	Pass	3 Spades	Pass
4 NT	Pass	5 Diamonds	Pass
5 NT	Pass	5 Spades	Pass
7 Spades	Pass	Pass	Pass

♣   ♥

In example 2, the declarer with 20 points opened 1 Spade and, when his partner jumped to 3 Spades calculated that his partner must have a minimum of 13 points. Their total points must be at least 33. The partnership is in the slam zone with Spades as the trump suit.

South uses the Blackwood convention to ask his partner for the Aces and the Kings. He found out that his team has all the Aces and all the Kings, so South decided to go to 7 Spades. If they were missing an Ace, or a King, he would have bid 6 Spades. If they were missing 2 top honors, he would have stopped at 5 Spades. You need to ask for the Aces and for the Kings, because counting your top honors is crucial when you bid for a slam.

Regardless what West leads, South will win the first trick and then collect the trumps in 2 rounds winning 2 tricks in trumps. South will win 2 tricks in Diamonds, 2 tricks in Clubs, and 3 tricks in Hearts by having the Dummy trump the ♥**7.** At the end he will win the 4 remaining trump tricks and makes his contract.

Example 3:

♠ Q 8 4
♥ K 9 8 2
♣ K J 6 2
♦ A 6

♠ A 7 3		North		♠ J 6 5
♥ 5 3				♥ 6 4
♣ Q 7 4 3	West		East	♣ 9 8 5
♦ 9 7 5 4		South		♦ J 10 8 3 2

♠ K 10 9 2
♥ A Q J 10 7
♣ A 10
♦ K Q

South (D)	West	North	East
1 Heart	Pass	3 Hearts	Pass
4 Clubs	Pass	4 Hearts	Pass
5 Clubs	Pass	5 Spades	Pass
6 Hearts	Pass	Pass	Pass

In example 3, South opened 1 Heart with 21 points, which is a high opener, and his partner jumped to 3 Hearts indicating an opening hand with minimum of 13 points. South did the math and knew that he and his partner were in the slam zone, with trump being Hearts. South and his partner use the Gerber convention. South bid 4 Clubs asking for Aces. North, with 1 Ace, responded 4 Hearts. South bid 5 Clubs

♣ ♥

asking for Kings. North, with 2 kings, responded 5 Spades.

South now knows that his team is missing 1 Ace, but they have the other 7 top honors (3 Aces + 4 Kings). He bids 6 Hearts.

West leads the ♠A and wins it. South will win the rest as follows: First collects the trumps in 2 rounds and wins 2 tricks in Hearts. Then wins 2 tricks in Diamonds, 2 tricks in Clubs, and 3 tricks in Spades. Then he wins the remaining 3 tricks in trumps and makes his contract.

Bridge Tip

Bidding slam in a suit is different than No Trumps. When you bid NT you only count the honor points and not the distribution points, but when you bid in a suit you count everything. This will make it tricky, because 33 or 37 points could be missing crucial honors. That's why you have to know how many Aces in your partner's hand, and sometimes how many Kings, before you go to slam.

Table 13: Slam Summary Table:

Slam	Requirement	
Small Slam- bid 6 (12 tricks)	33 Points	
Grand Slam- bid 7 (13 tricks)	37 Points	
NT Slam	No need to ask for Aces/Kings	
Suit Slam	Use Blackwood or Gerber convention to ask for Aces/Kings	
The Blackwood Convention	**Response**	
4 NT-Ask for Aces	5 Clubs: No Aces	
	5 Diamonds: One Ace	
	5 Hearts: Two Aces	
	5 Spades: Three Aces	
	5 Clubs: Four Aces	
5 NT-Ask for Kings	6 Clubs: No Kings	
	6 Diamonds: One King	
	6 Hearts: Two Kings	
	6 Spades: Three Kings	
	6 Clubs: Four Kings	
The Gerber Convention	**Response**	
4 Clubs-Ask for Aces	4 Diamonds: No Aces	
	4 Hearts: One Ace	
	4 Spades: Two Aces	
	4 NT: Three Aces	
	4 Diamonds: Four Aces	
5 Clubs-Ask for Kings	5 Diamonds: No Kings	
	5 Hearts: One King	
	5 Spades: Two Kings	
	5 NT: Three Kings	
	5 Diamonds: Four Kings	
Bonus Points	**Not Vulnerable**	**Vulnerable**
Small slam	500	750
Grand slam	1000	1500

Test yourself

Questions:

1. What's the easiest slam bid?

2. Why in No Trump slam is it unnecessary to ask for Aces?

3. How many points do you need to score small slam, and how many to score a grand slam?

4. In the Blackwood convention, which bid constitutes asking for Aces and which response means 2 Aces?

5. When do you receive slam bonus?

Answers:

1. No Trump.

2. Because you count only the honor points.

3. 33 for small slam, and 37 for grand slam.

4. 4 No Trumps to ask for Aces and a 5 Hearts response means 2 Aces.

5. When you bid and make a slam.

Playing Step 10

- In **step 10** playing the hand will require some preparations. First I recommend you actually read **step 10** and then have Table 13 "Slam Summary Table" on page 167 next to you. Last, set the cards to match the example on page 161.

- Bidding and scoring a slam requires the team on the offense to have 33 – 37 points. That's a lot of points, and doesn't happen very often. So, in order for us to practice bidding and playing a slam we have to pre-set the cards.

- Pre-set the cards to match example 1 and choose one team to be on the offense (South and North) and the other team to be on the defense (West and East). South will start the bidding by opening 1 NT, West will pass, and North will go to 6 NT. After three passes, West will lead and the playing of the hand will start. See if South and North were able to make their bid and score a small slam in NT.

- Pre-set the cards to match example 2 on page 162. Let the other team be on the offense and start the bidding as in example 2. The dealer will use the Blackwood convention when asking his partner for aces. When the bidding is complete, play the hand and see if the offense will score a grand slam in Spades.

- You can practice the Gerber convention by playing example 3 on page 164. Choose a different player to be South, and start bidding and playing the hand as in example 3. See if a small slam in Hearts is made.

- You can keep practicing those hands as often as you like by moving around the table and giving each player the chance to be South and bid for a slam.

THE LAST WORD

When playing Bridge, you play by the rules. You communicate with your partner through standard Bridge bidding that is known to all players on the table.

Everybody must speak the same Bridge language through bidding, so every team can have an equal chance to guess what the other team has.

If you want to use any artificial bids, like a short club or the Stayman Convention, which are explained below, you must declare that before the game starts and explain it to all players at the table.

Common Artificial Bids

Opening Short-Club:

When you and your partner agree not to play in a minor suit, you can open 1 Short-Club. Clubs and Diamonds are minor suits with low trick value. Spades and Hearts are major suits with higher trick value. Short-Club is an artificial bid that doesn't mean you have Clubs, but it means you have solid opening of 13-19 points and no 5 cards in a major suit. Playing Short-Club must be agreed upon with your partner before you start playing the game.

♠ A K 10 7	♠ A K J 9
♥ K Q 9 5	♥ A Q 10 7
♣ 10	♣ J 8 7
♦ K J 10 4	♦ 4 2

1 Short-Club   1 Short-Club

When you bid, you say 1 Club, not 1 Short-Club, your partner will understand that it is a Short-Club. Your partner is required to respond to you with his major suit of 4 cards or more. One Short-Club bid is a way for partners to find their best major suit. Their best major suit is one that is at least 8 cards between the two hands. It's only used when the opener doesn't have a 5 cards major suit to open with. Above are 2 examples of 1 Short-Club opening hand.

Bridge Tip

*Opening 1 Short-Club is an artificial bid requires 13-19 points. It is used when players prefer not to open in minor suits. They decide before the game starts to open **1 Club** as an artificial bid every time they don't have a major suit to open with. You respond to your partner with your major suit of 4 cards or more. 1 Short-Club is a way for the two partners to find an 8 card major suit to play in.*

Responding to 1 Short-Club:

You are required to respond to your partner with your major suit of 4 cards or more. 1 Short-Club is a way for the two partners to find an 8 cards suit to play in. It's only used when the opener doesn't have a 5 cards major suit to open with. The table on page 175 shows the Short-Club response.

The Stayman Convention:

The Stayman convention is an artificial bid in respond to 1 NT. If your partner opened 1 NT, you respond 2 Clubs asking your partner for his 4 card major suit. If the opener didn't have one, he replies 2 Diamonds. If he did, he responds 2 Hearts or 2 Spades.

Using the Stayman Convention is just like using Short-Club, or any other convention. It must be discussed in advance with your partner and the other players before playing the game.

Why would anyone want to use this convention at all? The reason is that it is generally advantageous for the "strong" hand to play the hand. For example, if the opening bid of INT was followed by a partner bid of 2 spades and the final contract ended up as 4 spades, the stronger hand would be Dummy. This give the opponents a better look at the strength of the partnership and gives them more information to play defense.

The Stayman Convention is popular in some bridge circles so you should be aware of it.

The table below shows you the Short-Club, and The Stayman convention:

Table 14: Response to Artificial Bids

Opening	Response	Comments
1 Short-Club (13-19) No 5 card major suit	7-10 points & 4 cards or more in a major suit: respond 1 in the major suit. 13-15 points: jump to the next level	An artificial bid, when you and your partner agree not to play in minor suits.
1 No Trump (16-18)	Respond to 1 NT using the Stayman Convention: Bid 2 Clubs asking the opener for his 4 cards major suit.	2 Clubs response is an artificial bid. It tells your partner that you don't have 5 cards major suit. At the same time it asks your partner for his 4 cards major suit. If your partner doesn't have a 4 cards major suit he'll respond with 2 Diamonds. If he has a major suit, he will respond in that major suit either 2 Hearts or 2 Spades.

Bridge Etiquette

Playing fair and not annoying or embarrassing any other player is all you need to know about Bridge etiquette.

The ACBL, American Contract Bridge League has zero tolerance policy against players who fail to uphold proper Bridge etiquette. The ACBL states that a player should refrain from:

♥ Paying insufficient attention.

♥ Making gratuitous comments during the play as to the auction or the adequacy of the contract.

♥ Detaching a card from the hand before it is that player's turn.

♥ Arranging the cards played to previous tricks in a disorderly manner or mixing the cards together before the result has been agreed to.

♥ Making a questionable claim or concession.

♥ Prolonging the play unnecessarily.

I strongly recommend using proper Bridge etiquette when playing with your friends and family at home. It makes the game much more enjoyable for everybody.

Special Etiquette Concerns for New Bridge Players:

There is a tendency to want to discuss a hand after it has been played. This is a great way for new bridge players to learn and improve their game - but be careful. Discussing can degenerate into criticism - real or imagined - that can spoil the evening. A few tips:

♥ Talk about discussing hands before the evening's play and get some agreement on "ground rules".

♥ Back off if you feel a member of your group is feeling uncomfortable or defensive. Talk about something else between hands.

♥ Always start the discussions referring to your own play or bidding, ie, "Do you think there was a better way for me to play that hand?", as opposed to, "If you lead a spade, I think we would have got them."

The Secret to winning in Bridge:

If football is a game of inches like they say, Bridge is a game of points. Even the card distribution is also converted into points. Your distribution and honor points are the indicators of the strength and the weakness of your hand.

You must only bid for a contract that you can afford. Think of your points as cash money in your pocket in a store that doesn't take checks or credit cards. You can only buy the items for which you have enough cash. If you try to buy an item for more than the cash you have, you'll be short and not get it. It's the same with Bridge contracts. If you don't have enough points to make the contract, you'll go down.

If points are like cash, then it's very important to be a smart shopper so you can get more for your money. Knowing how to properly use your points will maximize your winning.

After the bidding rounds are completed, both teams pretty much know how many points each team has. The challenge is in using those points and in the execution of your play whether on offense or defense

♠ ♦

If I can give you one simple piece of advise, one little secret about winning in Bridge, it would be to stick to the points requirement when bidding. This will lead to good communication with your partner, the right contract for your team, making your bids and ultimately winning in Bridge.

REFERENCE TABLES

Opening Bids

Opening	Points	Suit	Comments
1 suit (Low opening)	13- 15		Choose a major suit over a minor suit. If you have two equal major suits, bid the Heart first.
1 suit (High opening)	19-21	5 card suit	
2 suit (Demand bid)	21-25	5-7 card suit	Opening two is a demand bid. Your partner must not say pass until a game is reached.
3 suit (Pre-emptive)	6-10 Honor Points	7 card suit or longer	Count your quick tricks, and add 2 if vulnerable, or add 3 when not vulnerable.
1 No Trump	16-18	No void, no singleton. Three suits protected.	Balanced distribution 4-3-3-3, or 4-4-3-2, or 5-3-3-2
2 No Trump	22-24	No void, no singleton. Four suits protected.	Balanced distribution
3 No Trump	25-27	No void, no singleton. Four suits protected.	Balanced distribution
1 Short-Club	13-19	No 5 card major suit	An artificial bid, when you and your partner agree in advance not to play a minor suits.

♠ ♦

Table 2: Suit Response Bids

Opening	Response	Comments
1 suit (13-21)	6-10 points, and no biddable suit: bid 1 No Trump.	When you bid No Trump, count only the honors points, not the distribution points.
	6-10 points & 3 Trumps: respond 2 in the opening suit. 13-15 points: jump to the next level forcing a game.	Even if your partner has a low opening of 13 points, if you have 13 points that's 26 total, and enough for a game.
	7-10 points & 4 cards or more in a new suit: respond in the new suit. 13-15 points: jump up a level.	Choose a major suit over a minor suit. If you have two equal major suits, bid the lower rank first.
2 suit (21-25)	0-6 points: bid 2 No Trumps. 7 points plus: bid any Trump. You must keep responding until game is reached.	Opening two is a demand bid. You must not say pass even with 0 points.
3 suit (6-10)	7-10 points: pass, 13-15 points: respond 4 or 5 in the opening suit. (see Step 5)	Think that your partner can make 6-7 quick tricks. How many can you add from your hand?

NT Response Bids

Opening	Response	Comments
1 No Trump (16-18)	0-7 points, and long suit of 5+ cards: respond 2 in your long suit even with no honors. 10+ points: jump to 3 No Trump	Even if you have 0 points you must respond to 1 No Trump with your longest suit.
2 No Trump (22-24)	4-8 points: respond 3 No Trump	Even if your partner has 22 points, your team has enough for a game.
3 No Trump (25-27)	7 points: bid 4 No Trump, 8-11 points: bid 6 No Trump, 12 points: bid 7 No Trump.	Just add your points to your partner's points, and it will be easy to bid. 26 points are enough for 3 NT, with 33 points bid 6 NT, and with 37 points bid 7 NT.

Response to Artificial Bids

Opening	Response	Comments
1 Short-Club (13-19) No 5 card major suit	7-10 points & 4 cards or more in a major suit: respond 1 in the major suit. 13-15 points: jump to the next level	An artificial bid, when you and your partner agree not to play in minor suits.
1 No Trump (16-18)	Respond to 1 NT using the Stayman Convention: Bid 2 Clubs asking the opener for his 4 cards major suit.	2 Clubs response is an artificial bid. It tells your partner that you don't have 5 cards major suit. At the same time it asks your partner for his 4 cards major suit. If your partner doesn't have a 4 cards major suit he'll respond with 2 Diamonds. If he has a major suit, he will respond in that major suit either 2 Hearts or 2 Spades.

Re-Bid

Opening	Response	Opener re-bid	Responder re-bid
1 suit (13-21)	6-10 points, and no suit: bid 1 No Trump	Respond 2 in the opening suit	Pass
	6-10 points & 3 Trumps: respond 2 in the opening suit. 13-15 points: jump to the next level forcing a game	Add up your team points, if enough for a game, go to game. Otherwise pass, there is no benefit to raising the bid.	Pass
	7-10 points and 4 cards or more in a new suit: respond in the new suit. 13-15 points: jump to the next level	Play partner's new suit if you have 4 cards. Re-bid your opening suit if you have 6+ cards. Bid a secondary suit with 4+ card suit.	Make sure you don't leave your team playing a suit with less than 8 cards in Trump. If two suits are equal, choose the major suit.
2 suit (21-25)	0-6 points: bid 2 No Trumps. 7 points plus: bid any Trump. Must keep responding until game is reached	If your partner says 2 No Trump, go to your secondary suit	Go back to opening suit with 3+ cards. Bid the secondary suit with 4+ cards.
3 suit (6-10)	7-10 points: pass. 13-15 points: go to game	Pass	

Re-Bid, cont.

Opening	Response	Opener re-bid	Responder re-bid
1 No Trump (16-18)	0-7 points, and long suit of 5+ cards: respond 2 in your long suit even with no honors. 10+ points: jump to the next level.	With 2 suit respond, pass if you have 3 Trumps. If your partner jumps to the next level, go to game.	Pass
2 No Trump (22-24)	4-8 points: respond 3 No Trumps	Pass	Pass
3 No Trump (25-27)	7 points: bid 4 No Trumps. 8-11 points: bid 6 No Trumps. 12 points: bid 7 No Trumps	Against 4 No Trumps, pass or go to slam with 33 team points or more.	
1 Short-Club (13-15)	7-10 points and 4 cards or more in a major suit: respond 1 in the major suit. 13-15 points: jump to the next level	If you have 4+ cards in your partner suit, then make it the trump. Otherwise bid your secondary suit with 4+ cards.	With an 8 card sult, try a game or stay low depending on your points. If your team doesn't have 8 card suit, try No Trump.

Overcall Bid

Overcall	Suit	Comments	Response
1 suit (10-15 points): overcall at the 1st level.	5 card suit with 2+ top honors. (Aces, Kings, or Queens)	At the one level, you can overcall with as low as 10 points.	6-10 points and 3 Trumps: respond 2 in the overcall suit. 13-15 points: jump to the next level not forcing a game.
2 suit (13-15 points): overcall at the 2nd level.	5 card suit with 2+ top honors. (Aces, Kings, or Queens)	At the two level, you must have opening points to overcall.	6-10 points and 3 Trumps: respond 3 in the overcall suit. 13-15 points: go to game.
1 No Trump (16-18 points)	The opponent's opening suit must be well protected. It means you should have 1 or 2 sure winners in your opponent's opening suit.	You must be prepared to play it, if you have to. Also must have balanced distribution 4-3-3-3, or 4-4-3-2, or 5-3-3-2	0-7 points, and long suit of 5+ cards: respond 2 in your long suit even with no honors. 10+ points: jump to the next level.
Double (13-16 points) "Take-Out Double"	Support in the unbid suits. Or 5 card suit with 2+ top honors. (Aces, Kings, or Queens)	It's a call to your partner to name his best unbid suit. Preferably a major suit, and better stay at low level.	8-10 points, name your best unbid suit. Preferably a major suit. 8-10 points, with balanced distribution, and a stopper (sure winner) in the opponent's suit bid 1 No Trump. 13+ points: go to game.

Overcall Bid, continued

Overcall	Suit	Comments	Response
3 suit or more (pre-emptive), (6-10 points) plus 7+ cards in one suit. Usually to stop your opponents from scoring a second game and winning the rubber.	7+ card suit	Before you bid, count your quick tricks, and add 2 if vulnerable*, or add 3 when not vulnerable*. Might get a double, and might go down.	7-10 points: pass. 13-15 points: go to game.

Lead Card - Suit Contract

Condition	Cards	Suit	Lead
If your partner made a bid, lead in your partner's suit. If you have two honors in your partner's suit, play the highest. If you have 1 honor, play the lowest card except if the honor is the Ace. Always play the Ace.	If you have an Ace in your partner's suit.	AXX	Ace
	2 card suit, or 2 card sequence, play the highest	J10	J
	3 card sequence, play the highest	KQJ	K
	3 card suit headed by 2 honors, play the highest	QJX	Q
	4 card suit headed by 2 honors, play the highest	KQXX	K
	1 honor in a 3 or 4 card suit, play the lowest.	KXX	X
If your partner has not made a bid. The rule still applies. If you have two honors in a suit, play the highest. If you have 1 honor, play the lowest card. In this case you don't always play the Ace. If you have AQX, don't play the Ace. You might win 2 tricks if you wait.	2 card suit, or 2 card sequence, play the highest	AK	Ace
	3 card sequence, play the highest	KQJ	K
	1 honor in a 3 or 4 card suit, play the lowest.	KXX	X
	Ace, Queen sequence	AQX	Do not lead this suit

♣

Lead Card - NT Contract

Condition	Cards	Suit	Lead
If your partner has not made a bid. Lead your own suit. If you don't have a suit, lead in the Dummy's bid suit that declarer didn't respond to.	Lead the 4th highest from your longest suit	QJ9732	7
	Lead the lowest from 3 or 4 card suit.	Q105	5
	Lead the highest from 2 card suit.	J9	J

Slam Summary Table:

Slam	Requirement
Small Slam- bid 6 (12 tricks)	33 Points
Grand Slam- bid 7 (13 tricks)	37 Points
NT Slam	No need to ask for Aces/Kings
Suit Slam	Use Blackwood or Gerber convention to ask for Aces/Kings
The Blackwood Convention	**Response**
4 NT-Ask for Aces	5 Clubs: No Aces
	5 Diamonds: One Ace
	5 Hearts: Two Aces
	5 Spades: Three Aces
	5 Clubs: Four Aces
5 NT-Ask for Kings	6 Clubs: No Kings
	6 Diamonds: One King
	6 Hearts: Two Kings
	6 Spades: Three Kings
	6 Clubs: Four Kings
The Gerber Convention	**Response**
4 Clubs-Ask for Aces	4 Diamonds: No Aces
	4 Hearts: One Ace
	4 Spades: Two Aces
	4 NT: Three Aces
	4 Diamonds: Four Aces
5 Clubs-Ask for Kings	5 Diamonds: No Kings
	5 Hearts: One King
	5 Spades: Two Kings
	5 NT: Three Kings
	5 Diamonds: Four Kings
Bonus Points	**Not Vulnerable**	**Vulnerable**
Small slam	500	750
Grand slam	1000	1500

Downs Value

Downs	Not Vulnerable			Vulnerable		
	Un-doubled	Doubled	Re-Doubled	Un-doubled	Doubled	Re-Doubled
1	50	100	200	100	200	400
2	100	300	600	200	500	1000
3	150	500	1000	300	800	1600
4	200	800	1600	400	1100	2200
5	250	1100	2200	500	1400	2800
6	300	1400	2800	600	1700	3400
7	350	1700	3400	700	2000	4000
8	400	2000	4000	800	2300	4600
9	450	2300	4600	900	2600	5200
10	500	2600	5200	1000	2900	5800
11	550	2900	5800	1100	3200	6400
12	600	3200	6400	1200	3500	7000
13	650	3500	7000	1300	3800	7600

Tricks Value

Tricks	Not Vulnerable			Vulnerable		
	Un-doubled	Doubled	Re-Doubled	Un-doubled	Doubled	Re-Doubled
Club	20	40	80	20	40	80
Diamond	20	40	80	20	40	80
Heart	30	60	120	30	60	120
Spade	30	60	120	30	60	120
1st No Trump	40	80	160	40	80	160
No Trump	30	60	120	30	60	120
Over Tricks	Trick value	100	200	Trick value	200	400
Bonus for making a doubled contract: 50						

Bonus Points

Plays	Bonus
Rubber 2-0 game	700
Rubber 2-1 game	500
Unfinished rubber (1 game)	300
Partial game score	50
4 honors, A K Q J in one suit*	100
5 honors, A K Q J 10 in one suit*	150
4 Aces when playing No Trump	150

* When playing that suit

Slam Bonus

Slam - Bid and Made	Not Vulnerable	Vulnerable
Small slam (12 tricks)	500	750
Grand slam (13 tricks)	1000	1500

Glossary

Blackwood Convention - An artificial bid used in slam bidding and starts at the 4 No Trumps level. It's used to ask your partner for the number of Aces and the number of Kings in his hand.

Book - Winning the 1st 6 tricks by the Declarer.

Contract - A promise to win a specific number of tricks.

Dealer - The player whose turn it is to deal the cards.

Declarer - The winner of the bidding and the one that will play the hand.

Doubleton - Holding two cards of any suit.

Dummy - The declarer's partner that lays down his cards.

Finesse - Turning your opponent's winning card into a loser.

Game - Bidding and making 100 points or more.

Gerber Convention - An artificial bid used in slam bidding and starts at the 4 Clubs level. It's used to ask your partner for the number of Aces and the number of Kings in his hand.

Grand slam - Bidding and winning 7 in a suit or 7 in No Trump. That's 13 tricks which is all the tricks in the hand.

Hand - The hand is the playing of the cards after they are dealt.

Honors - The 4 honors in every suit are the Ace, King, Queen, and the Jack. Sometimes the 10 is called the 5th honor.

Jump - Bid higher than the immediate next level.

Long suit - 6 cards or longer

Major suit - Spades or Hearts.

Minor suit - Clubs or Diamonds.

No Trump - Playing without a trump suit.

Not Vulnerable - The team that has not won a game yet is called "not vulnerable".

Opening bid - The 1st bid.

Opening lead - The 1st card led before the Dummy lay down his cards.

Opening points - 13 or more points.

Overtrick - Winning an extra trick over the contracted number of tricks.

Pre-emptive bid - A high opening bid designed to discourage the opponents from bidding.

Protected suit - A suit where you have winners.

Round - When every player has played a card.

Rubber - A set of two games won by one team.

Short-Club - An artificial bid designed to ask your partner for his major suit of 4 cards or more.

Singleton - Holding one card of any suit.

Small slam - Bidding and winning 6 in a suit or 6 in No Trump. That is 12 tricks which is all the tricks in the hand except one.

Stayman Convention - An artificial bid in response to I No Trump. You bid two Clubs to ask your partner for his best 4 card major suit.

Stoppers - Sure winners in the opponents bid suit.

Trick - A round of play where each player played a card.

Trick winner - The player that won the trick using a high card or Trump.

Trump - The suit bid for the contract.

Void - Holding no cards of a suit.

Vulnerable - The team that won their first game is called "vulnerable".

Winners - Cards that you feel sure will win tricks in any given hand.

About the Author

Samir Riad was born in Cairo, Egypt and earned his bachelors degree in Electrical Engineering from the HIT High Institute of Technology in Helwan, Egypt. His passion for math and physics was only surpassed by his passion for playing Bridge. He would very often stay up all night playing Bridge with his friends. Over the years, he taught many friends how to play the game and was often amazed at how quickly their intimidation diminished and how enthusiastic they became. It was because of this that Samir felt so driven to write this book. His unique teaching method is simple and he hopes it will bring many more people into the incredibly enjoyable world of Bridge playing.

Samir moved to California in 1985 and became a citizen in 1990. He has owned a chain of wireless cellular phone stores in the San Francisco Bay Area for more than 20 years and currently lives with his wife and children in San Jose, California.

STMRY
Gift
$14.39

8379046R0

Made in the USA
Lexington, KY
31 January 2011